THE MUSIC STARTED AND THE RAFTERS ROCKED!

Used to be that everyone thought Ath__ __ __ece. But then in the late seventies came The B-52's, a "tacky little dance band from Georgia," whose lead singer was a little guy with a necktie and a pencil-thin mustache. Soon the kids in town were becoming aware of the new do-it-yourself music movement. They began to feel and see that they were a part of it. Suddenly Athens, this nowhere Georgia hick town, was *the* Athens where it all was at. The 40 Watt Club became the epicenter of the weekend nighttime downtown scene. During the shows, when the dancing hit full-steam, the owners would run downstairs to the closed sandwich shop and wedge two-by-fours against the rafters to keep the floor from collapsing. One night someone brought a thermometer to the R.E.M. show and it topped 125 degrees. That was normal. The formal Athens music scene had begun. . .

PARTY OUT OF BOUNDS

Rodger Lyle Brown grew up in Savannah and lived in Athens from 1977 to 1987. He has worked as editorial director for Playboy.com and Britannica.com, contributed to publications ranging from **The New York Times Magazine** to the **Village Voice**, and is the author of *Ghost Dancing on the Cracker Circuit: The Culture of Festivals in the American South.*

Also by Rodger Lyle Brown:
Ghost Dancing on the Cracker Circuit:
The Culture of Festivals in the American South.

RodGEr LylE bRown

paRTy OUt of BOUNds

THE B-52'S,
R.E.M.
AND THE
KIDS WHO
ROCKED
ATHENS,
GEORGIA

everthemore
B O O K S

The author extends grateful acknowledgement to Night Garden Music for permission to excerpt lyrics from Bad Day, Shaking Through, and Mystery to Me.

Library of Congress Cataloging in Publication Data:

Brown, Rodger Lyle.
    Party out of bounds : the B-52's, R.E.M. and the kids who rocked
    Athens, Georgia / Rodger Lyle Brown.
    ISBN 0-9743877-0-3
    1. Rock music--Georgia--Athens--History and criticism. 2. Rock
    groups--Georgia--Athens. 3. B-52s (Musical Group) 4. R.E.M.
    (Musical Group) I. Title

This book was originally published in 1991 by Plume, an imprint of New American Library, a division of Penquin Books, USA

This edition published in 2003 by everthemore books.

everthemore books
484 C Moreland Avenue
Atlanta, GA 30307

www.everthemorebooks.com
866-681-5128

Cover design by Shari Moore
Cover photos by Linda Hopper

To the memory of
Richard Louis Brown, Sr.

ACKNOWLEDGMENTS

Many people contributed encouragement during the research-ing, writing and rewriting of this book. Many also contributed useful stories, muddled libels, yellowed clippings, dirty photo-graphs, subtle chiding, and vicious mockery. Some said I was undertaking an impossible chore. Others said I was cutting my own throat by trying to write about a small town of close friends and intimate lunatics. Maybe so. But to all of these people in various degrees I owe thanks. Here's my list, in no particular order:

The righteous sister Sandra-Lee Phipps, Phyllis Stapler, Ann Boyles, Linda Hopper, Leslie Michel, Mike Green, Ken Tapscott, Kevin Dunn, Tom Smith, Craig Woodall, Jerry Ayers, Peter Buck, Mike Mills, Michael Stipe, Bill Berry, Jefferson Holt, Bertis Downs, Liz Hammond, Dana Downs, Dan Wall, Rick "the Printer" Hawkins, Ken Buck, Randy Bewley, Curtis Crowe, Michael Lachowski, Jim Herbert, Jackie (Slayton) Methe, John

Methe, Mike Huff, Kate Pierson, Cindy Wilson, Keith Bennett, Fred Schneider, Keith Strickland, Robert Waldrop, Tommy Adams, Angel Dean, Mark Schone, Vic Varney, David Gamble, Armistead Wellford, Mark Cline, Mike Richmond, Andrew Carter, John Seawright, Sam Seawright, Danny Beard, Tony Paris, Tony Eubanks, William Orten Carlton, Ann States, Ingrid Schorr, David Pierce, Kathleen O'Brien, Neill Bogan, Nicky Giannaris, Kit Swarz, Steve "Boat Of roadie" May, Debi Heidel, Chuck Searcy, Chris Short, Cliff Bostock, Amy Walter, and my editor, Christopher Schelling. And a hey and a thanks to Wendy Malloy. And thanks to the Friday lunch at Tortillas, featuring Sheri Hodges, Rob. Walton, and the inimitable John "Chowder Shouter" Thomas. And a salutary nod to the brotherhood: Harlan Hale, David Helmey, Paul Lombard, and Joe Kuhl.

A special thanks must go to Vanessa (Briscoe, Ellison) Hay, for knowing my name at the right time; and Leslie Currie, for knowing much more.

Contents

PART TWO: SPEAKERS IN THE WINDOW; SPRINKLERS IN THE YARD

Way back in 1989, I was working at a newspaper in Atlanta, and I came back from lunch to find a message on my desk. It was from a literary agent in New York City. The subject line was provocative: "Discuss an idea for a book."

I assumed she meant doing a book review, but when I returned her call, I discovered, much to my surprise, that she was suggesting that I might be interested in writing a book. She said she'd gotten my name from a friend of hers. This friend had reported to her that I had lived in Athens during the late 70s and most of the 80s and was now working as a writer. She said a publishing company was looking for a book about "this Athens thing," and she asked me to write a proposal.

I said sure.

Weeks later, I had a book contract to write what the New York editor wanted to call "The Golden Age of Athens."

"You know, like with Greece," he said. "We think it's great!"

I thought it was horrible.

Eventually we settled on "Party Out of Bounds."

I wrote the book. It was published. And then began the standard story: publishing company promises six-city tour and national advertising in Rolling Stone, but when all was said and done, my grand book tour consisted of a trip to

Minneapolis where I did two early-morning radio interviews. That was the extent of the promotion. I got more ink from Matthew Sweet complaining about his description in the book than I did from any of the promised co-op advertising.

But then a strange thing began to happen. By the late 1990s, I was working for Playboy in Chicago, and I began to get emails from people looking for copies of the book. They all had stories to tell: They had read it a long time ago, but their sister had swiped it. Or they used to have a copy but gave it away when they moved and always regretted it. Or a friend of theirs was a huge B-52's fan and they wanted to give them the book as a graduation gift.

You can imagine my surprise to discover that anybody still remembered the book. And they actually had fond memories of it. I would have sent them copies, but, alas, I had none. *Party Out of Bounds* was out of print.

Now, thanks to everthemore books, *Party Out of Bounds: The B-52's, R.E.M. and the Kids Who Rocked Athens, Ga.* is back in print, and it will always be available for current and future generations who want to read about life in Athens, Georgia, way back when.

What you hold in your hands today is a reasonable facsimile of the original. The cover and design are different, some of the photos are different and the stock is different. Peter Buck no longer lives in the house mentioned in the prologue, but other than that, it's the same book that you would have bought back in 1991, if you had actually bought it back then.

Rodger Lyle Brown
Atlanta, 2003

"Does not the true character of each epoch come alive in the nature of its children?"

—KARL MARX

"It's been a bad day, please don't take my picture."

—MICHAEL STIPE

PREFACE

What follows here is a conjured history of the Athens, Georgia, music scene. It's a tale of a small southern college town and the run of kids and not-kids through its streets, through space and time. It's a story of a couple dozen rock-and-rollers and their struggles for fame—some of whom made it, some of whom didn't. It's a book-length folktale that I have spun up out of the slush and muck of many gathered half-remembered and misbegotten memories. It's equal parts cultural anthropology, cosmetic surgery, elegiac memoir, and conspiracy theory: hence its characterization as a conjuration.

The story spans nearly a decade, during which time, by my quick and unofficial calculation, about fifty thousand new students passed through town to attend, haunt, or subvert the University of Georgia. Only a very few of them ever participated in the "scene," but even those few equal quite a number. Through the years many people showed their faces, sounded their voices, and involved their bodies in the many plots and subplots which roam in the flux of gossip. All of those stories are very interesting but, due to a number of constraints, I have had to neglect them for the more "historically relevant" tales of the few.

Apologies to the disappeared.

To gather the material for this book I interviewed dozens of Athens' current and erstwhile citizens. The result of that effort was hundreds of hours of oral history. Much of it was useful and insightful; most of it was glorified myth, or vague and confused renditions of overheard stories passed off as eyewitness accounts, the legends repeated so often that the storytellers finally convinced themselves that they were really there. I have taken that stuff and spiked it with my own remembrances of living there from 1977 to 1987. What I ended up with is an overview history of the new music bands that started in Athens, beginning with The B-52's. In the course of telling that history, I have also tried to recreate the feeling of living in a small hick Georgia college town in those fast and frantic first years after punk.

The result of all this tale-telling is folklore, documented gossip. It's a yarn like what you'd hear if you sat up late in some Athens kitchen talking with old friends about the past. Some folks might tell the story differently, but this is how I've heard it.

PROLOGUE

In Athens, Georgia, a Victorian mansion built in 1889 stands on a dead-end street in the historic neighborhood of Cobbham. It's huge, ornate, the best on the block. Today it's the home of Peter Buck, guitarist for R.E.M. In the late 1970s however, the house was haven to a half-dozen of Athens' transient art students. Paint-stained and black-coated mystics who read too much Jean Genet rigged their studio-shelters in the sprawling rooms. They blanketed the floors with salvaged rags and braced their much-abused mattresses with overdue library books. The glass in the windows was cracked and broken. The boards on the porch were rotten and split. The crumbling walls were spray-painted "Jimi Hendrix is God," and a lost little girl nobody knew slept during the day in an attic alcove and was only seen at night, smoking filterless cigarettes outside on the widow's walk.

But that's all changed. Peter owns the house now. It's been immaculately restored: new sheetrock, new plaster, light bulbs in all the fixtures. At night every room is lit, and the glimmer from the windows illuminates the new paint job. The irony of the house's new condition is not lost on the former tenants. Those still around, they remember what the place used to look like. They remember the Athens before anybody was famous. These days, they often walk down to the close of that dead-end street to recollect party stories and show new friends where they once lived. They stand at the edge of the yard, look up at the door of etched glass sparkling from the light within, and mumble in wistful admiring disbelief.

"Back when I lived there, rent was only twenty bucks a month. *And R.E.M. sucked!*"

Nobody ever thought, back then, that Peter Buck, a typical rock-and-roll, floor-sleeping bad boy, would end up in his thirties collecting folk art and Memphis plastic, filling fast the rooms of that Victorian mansion with handmade musical instruments and books shipped by caravan from bazaars, airport bookstores, and hotel lobbies around the world. Nobody thought his band would be so successful. *"They just play rock and roll!"* But here he is a decade later, the one-time sneering knifehandler, now faced with the quandary of what to do with his fortune, wondering if he should invest in rental properties.

Back when Peter's house was still a wreck and not yet his, Michael Stipe, singer for the band, walked the streets of Athens with his hair streaked blond-red-orange and got regularly drenched with beer thrown by frat boys shouting "fag" from passing cars. Now, just as Peter owns a Cobbham mansion, Michael is no longer a pariah, a henna-headed playtime poorboy. He's a culture star. The little brothers and sisters of his tormentors buy R.E.M. CDs and albums, turning them into platinum and gold. They pay twenty bucks a pop to see him sing his hits and shadow-box in stretch tights. In the transit from then to now, Michael Stipe has gone from iconoclast to icon. Weird wandering seekers come to Athens from across the country, moist-eyed, seeking his benefaction. Runaway girls and enraptured gentle-boy poets crowd the streets and stake out his house with video cameras secreted in their rucksacks. Michael's love of folk art has caused the Georgia countryside to be picked clean of hand-lettered "Boil'd P-nut" signs by well-meaning imitators in baggy pants and muddy Chinese slippers.

By anyone's reckoning, he's made it.

In 1988, eight years after debuting in the back of an old desanctified Athens church, R.E.M. was put on the cover of *Rolling Stone* and declared by that industry standard to be America's Best Rock-and-Roll Band. That year they were freed from their contract with I.R.S. Records after putting out *Document*, their fifth album and the first to sell a million. They soon signed with Warner Bros., and after the release of *Green*, *Rolling Stone* again gave them the cover, this time calling them America's hippest band. They'd done it; they'd reached the toppermost of the poppermost. And through it all they'd stayed in Athens, that little southern town that saw their birth.

As a result, Athens ain't what she used to be.

It's not easy to accommodate international celebrity in a small town, especially one like Athens where the middle-class college kids who crowd its streets have been teethed on the ideology of fame. And the members of R.E.M.—Mike Mills, Bill Berry, Michael Stipe, Pete Buck—are international celebrities. The students are aware of it, but they try and keep cool. At clubs and bars, sightings of any member of R.E.M. are reported through crowds by a subtle communal alarm, the same instinct that choreographs the fits and starts of a school of fish.

It's nothing more than an overheard murmuring of a name (*"Mike Mills!" "Bill Berry!"*) and the quick snap of a head turning toward the door. With that, the room becomes aware, electrified. The cooler kids don't show their unease. They almost swagger, confident that they will get a nod or a pat on the shoulder, being tapped out for membership in an honorary society of those who have touched the human face of God. Tourist kids, those young ones from other college campuses across the country who've come to Athens like Moslems for a weekend in Mecca, are especially alert and nervous. "They're here. They're in this room with me!" For so long the members of R.E.M. have been nothing but idols of paper and vinyl to them, two-dimensional culture heroes made of script and soundtrack. But now, here they are. They appear in the flesh.

While the visiting Iowa-boys and Jersey-girls wait for one of the guys to walk by, these eager teenage acolytes, certified hip by their fake IDs and Marlboro Lights, grip long-neck beer bottles a little tighter, roll moist napkins into tight spirals around their fingers, and flick sideways glances. When they finally see one of the guys, all is well. They can breathe again. And around the edge of whatever crowded barroom, the jaded ones who've been around for a while, who've watched history happen, sit snide and sly, smirk at the panic, the fawning, and mutter into their drinks: "It's R.E.M.'s world. Isn't it nice they let us live here?"

It wasn't always that way. Used to be everyone thought Athens was in Greece. But then in the late seventies came The B-52's, that "tacky little dance band from Georgia." The B-52's ignited the Athens music scene by jamming their dance rock in a southern boogie town. They put the place on the map. But then they left. They moved to New York. And in their wake came up a generation of original bands that have made rock-and-roll history: Pylon, The Method Actors, Love Tractor, R.E.M.

And in Athens, that history of Georgia's original agrarian punk has settled into a folklore that is repeated regularly by the one-time kids when on Sunday mornings they sit around kitchen tables cluttered with coffee cups and loose tobacco. There, in the tree-shaded wood-frame houses, those old scenemaker folk recapitulate the creation myth, remembering what they can of those years full of forgotten weekends when beer was lifeblood, acid was candy, and three days so easily became smeared into one.

They retell what they've seen, repeat what they've heard. Somebody tells about when The B-52's were still in town, innocently strutting their glam-rock drag in the middle of the street. Someone else recalls the time quaaludes were bountiful and the neighborhood sidewalks turned into Möbius strips. Another pantomimes the night Michael Stipe fell off the stage at the nightclub Tyrone's and barely crawled back up. Finally everybody hoots about the time a local character called Brother Dave did too much uncooked MDA and spent a whole party thrashing in the front yard of the punk girls' house out on the highway across from the Putt Putt miniature golf course, bleeding from the ears while his buddy Brother Mike stood over him with a pony keg of Pabst Blue Ribbon tucked under his arm, pouring free beer for the girls.

Those left in town, adults now, talk about how it's not like the old days. They can't party like they used to. And besides, even if they could, it just isn't the same anymore.

They shake their heads and wonder how they ever survived.

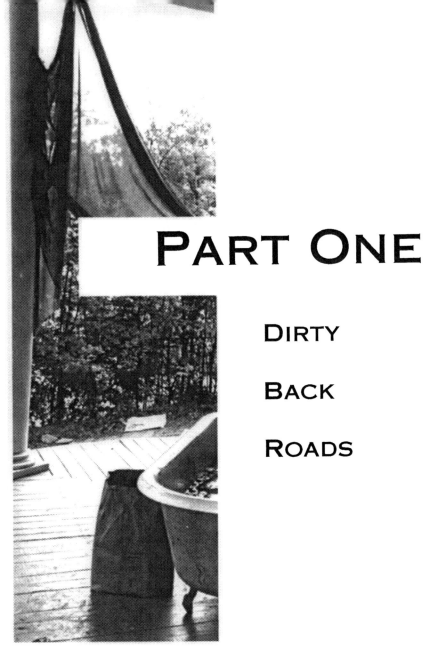

PART ONE

DIRTY

BACK

ROADS

THE FOUNDING FATHERS CRASH A PARTY — A SCHOOL IS STARTED — THE PARABLE OF THE IRON HORSE — KEITH STRICKLAND MEETS FRED SCHNEIDER

In 1801, five men in dusty breeches and leather boots rode up into what was no longer Indian Country but what, a few years earlier, had become the latest addition to the young state of Georgia. This new territory spread from the Appalachee River in the west to the Savannah River in the east. North to south it stretched from the foothills of the Blue Ridge Mountains to the sandhill lowlands of the Coastal Plain. It was a massive swath of hills and hardwood forests, got by musket and treaty from the Cherokee and the Creek Indians. Once possession was secured, it doubled the size of the state.

A few years earlier the state assembly was flush with the new independence from Britain and drafted a charter for a university. As an endowment for the school, the legislators set aside five five-thousand-acre parcels of land in the new counties. With that act they made their yet-unbuilt University of Georgia the first land-grant university in America.

The assembly opened the land to settlers, who steadily rode into the area with a willingness to cut trees, clear land, and fight off the dispossessed Indians, who quickly regretted their fateful and easy cession. There was no lack of new Americans, dislocated during the Revolution, eager to trek into the wilderness. And so they came. During the next two decades they tore violently from the land their plantations and farms.

Although the state had decided to start a school in 1785, it wasn't until 1800 that the political finagling was finished and the "Senatus Academicus" named a committee to go and look for a site. That next year, 1801, once the spring rains ended, the group of five men rode into the once-wild, now-settled Indian Country. The five men who rode up into that land were all notable Georgians who would one day give their names to their state's counties, towns and streets: Baldwin, Milledge, Walton, Twiggs, Lawson.

They rode the old Indian trading trail for a week, scouting locations in the low end of Jackson County. On July 3 they spent the night at a tavern near the county line. On the morning of the fourth they woke early and rode out and up into a ridge of hills between the Middle Oconee and the Oconee rivers.

They came to the wide, granite-bottomed shallows at Cedar Shoals on the Oconee River, where a group of settlers had gathered under the trees along the riverbank to celebrate America's independence. The rum was warm. They made their own music. They sang the old revolutionary hymns. Inadvertantly that day, the committee of five set a tone that has since resonated throughout the history of the Georgia town that has since come to be called the Liverpool of the South and the Land of a Thousand Dances:

They crashed the party.

After making introductions the site selection committee spent the rest of the day lifting mugs of rum and beer in toast to the Senatus Academicus that had sent them on their mission up into the old Indian Country. They toasted the new nation and its constitution. They toasted liberty. They toasted Josiah Meigs, who would be the university's first president and would graciously give his name to one of the meanest streets of the soon-to-be town. They toasted freedom and all that went with it.

The five had such a good time at the party, and so felt the magic of the spot, that the next day they decided that there, near those tranquil clear-running shoals on a set of hills on a bend in the Oconee River, they would build their new academy.

It was the perfect site: fields of corn, cotton, and potatoes flanked the recently cleared hillsides. Clear water bubbled from springs. Livestock grazed the slopes. Apple and peach orchards were already planted and the rivers were full of fish, even though it was mostly shad, an easy breed common to the meandering fresh water. Few noxious vapors rose from the swampy lowland by the rivers, and what little there was blew away eastward with the favorable winds. The decision made, the committee acquired the land, let the contracts for the wood-, stone-, and brickwork for the first building of the university. They laid out lots for a town that would become the cradle for the state's high culture and the playground for generations of its young.

They knew all along what they would name it: Athens.

Today when you drive out of Athens the countryside spreads itself green and red and brown: settled, but rural still. Fields along the road are bordered by three-strand barbed wire. The cotton, once king, is gone now. The fields are planted in corn and soil healing soybeans. Cows graze. Where the fields and pasture aren't shave-cut to reveal the rolling topography of these uplands, the forest comes almost to the edge of the road: sometimes thick hardwood, but mostly the fast-growing pine: timberland done in straight, machine-planted rows that run up and over the slow hills, rows that blink and strobe as you speed by; rows that the paper company comes and clear-cuts maybe once every twenty years for pulpwood and telephone poles.

You drive along. . . . Houses and yards come cut out of the

forests and the fields: white clapboard, gray asphalt-sided, quick-rigged brick ranch-style with a mother-in-law trailer. Some yards are lawns, lush green. Others are packed dirt, kept bald and head-cracking hard by bounced basketballs, rolling dogs, and scrambling kids. Around the sides of some of the houses, as you get out past eight, ten miles, are an outdoor well and a tank of propane gas; a parked new pickup, an aging Le Baron: a rusty, once-candy-striped swingset.

Go still farther out . . . and you're past any threat of suburb. You enter the realm where roving feral dogs feed on wildlife killed on the road and dumped in ditches. Out there, old share-cropper shacks come up from the brambles and kudzu, gray-planked, *tin-roof-rusted*, falling in from broken center beams, some already fallen all the way to leaving just a crumbled clay-brick chimney. Out that far the tract houses stop. It seems a wilderness on both sides but for the pavement, the speed-limit signs, and the churches, which appear more frequently than stoplights along the two-lane, out-there highways that lace the once-wild Georgia countryside and strap it down.

It's all what you would expect, but going south on Highway 15, out of Athens and through Watkinsville (where stands the tavern that lodged the university search committee two hundred years ago), there is an incongruous sight, one that serves as an object lesson to explain the cultural climate that prevailed in Athens for the first two hundred years of the town's history and sets the stage for what would happen as the 1970s ran out, down and up into the eighties, when the whole Athens music thing took off:

In a field, across the road from a sandpit on Highway 15, there stands an iron horse:

If you are a student at the University of Georgia, at some point in the four-or-more-year sojourn through college that the usual student makes, you somehow find out about that horse. It stands on a low rise, miles out of town, and in the fall, let's say at a full moon, you ride out there. It's far enough out of town that the car ride becomes a trip in itself, without any chemical aid. Once gone from town and into the dark, empty countryside, you drive along and after a bit find yourself on the edge of the Oconee Forest. There, in the field, off to the left, stands the horse.

On that clear night (you choose the night) you leave the car and walk out there, keeping a hold on whomever you're with. Together you list from side to side and trip across the cut stalks and huge, disc-disturbed dirt clods. You hear dogs barking, alert somewhere in farmyards down the road, through the woods. You keep telling each other that the dogs are too far away to be barking at *ya'll*. Trying to convince yourselves you're safe, you repeat to each other, giggling, tripping, that nobody knows you're there.

You cross the field, walking from the road, and you get to the horse. The iron gives off its cold. All around you is nothing but a slowly rolling field of cut corn. You see the dark edge of the forest's beginning on the other side of the river. You see the strip of the highway that hosts your car, parked leaning on the shoulder, angling into the thick grass of the ditch, separated from the field by only the low boundary fence of three-strand barbed wire. You climb on the horse, sit and share cigarettes, pass on the lore, telling about how you first found this incongruous statue. You look up at the thickness of stars and talk about how weird it is that there's this iron horse out in the middle of a corn field on the edge of the Oconee Forest, ten miles outside of Athens.

The horse is an abstract sculpture commissioned in the fifties by the University of Georgia. At the time, the notable annual events in Athens were an International Livestock Show and the American Legion Carnival. The horse sculpture was the result of an effort to encourage the fine arts. But the statue wasn't anything like the town-square style tributes to Robert E. Lee, that hero of the Old South rearing back on Traveller, man and horse clad with the flesh and semblance of real life befitting works of art.

The piece was "abstract," or so the more sophisticated locals called it, welded so that the guts were visible gears, looking like a cubist doodle cast in two tons of iron. Its ribs were few and it stood six feet at the shoulder.

When the work was finished the university found a site for it: an empty rectangle of worn dirt that served as play and parade ground for the students who lived in the Reed and Payne Hall dormitories. The university set aside a spare few feet for the horse, but when it was set on its pedestal in the middle of a perfectly good softball field, the students would have none of it.

One night pranksters stacked wood underneath the work and set the pile afire. A few days later they hung a bag of oats over the horse's head, swaddled the sculpture in diapers made from bed sheets, and piled the ground around it with manure. The students issued statements that they didn't want art in the middle of their quad. It was a monstrosity, a foreign, urban-derived hallucination. It was *"mod'ren art,"* the work of some *"feygit"* imagination. In the fifties, the students at the University of Georgia weren't as open to artistic deviance as they would become.

Finally, they rioted.

The artist in resident who made the thing protested to the administration about the mistreatment of his work. The school cast around for a way to get rid of the sculpture. The only place they could find for a two-ton iron horse cut in a modernist design was ten miles outside of town in the middle of a field on a rise just this side of the Oconee River on Highway 15. They put the horse there, and there it still stands.

That was the cultural atmosphere in the little southern town as it entered the modern age.

Things changed slowly during the sixties. There was scattered stone-throwing to protest desegregation and the war in Vietnam. The ROTC building was spray-painted "Che Lives" and then blown up. In 1969 a day of protest against the war was held, and

Governor Lester Maddox (the Georgia governor best known for chasing blacks from his fried-chicken restaurant with an ax handle) condemned the protestors as traitors and, while he was at it, condemned desegregation as "sick." While the war in Vietnam was protested by a handful of activists, the fraternities collected skin-mags to airlift to the boys in the Southeast Asian combat zone, and the sororities solicited candidates for the Maid of Cotton contest. During a Derby Day celebration, one gang of overexcited sorority girls accidentally crushed a pig and were made to promise never to do it again.

On the art front the students demanded that more rock bands be brought to campus. "Led Zeppelin, not the Lettermen," they chanted during one lunchtime protest. The university union responded. When Henry Mancini canceled an appearance, the union booked Iron Butterfly in his stead.

In February 1969 a significant cultural advance was made. A student club called Dante's Domain opened in the basement of Memorial Hall on campus. Memorial Hall had been built in the 1920s as a tribute to the boys' blood sacrificed in World War I. Bands played at Dante's and it quickly became a hangout for both students and kids from town. It was there that the germ of rockthrill was laid down in Athens. Unfortunately, things got carried away at one show as the kids ran through the hallways of the building, trashing tables, tearing up carpets, smoking "grass" in the janitor's closet. The administration was scandalized. By the end of 1969 Dante's was under scrutiny for giving the University Union a bad name due to the "freaks and longhairs" who hung out there. As the seventies began, it was converted back to a coffee house featuring acoustic folk music and a sit-down crowd.

Dante's was suppressed, but local kids kept coming onto campus to feel the heat of the thousands of students at critical mass. One spring day in the early seventies while Nixon was still president, Keith Strickland, a local kid, walked onto campus with some of his friends to check out a band that was playing on the

plaza in front of Memorial Hall. At that time fraternity and sorority kids were still clipped in khaki and oxford cloth, and the
free-boy hippies went barefoot and shirtless, wore mustaches and
long, lank hair; the straight-haired earth mamas wore bells, halter
tops, and peasant dresses.

Unlike everyone else in town, Keith was into the stacked
heels of the latest thing—glitter rock.

On that spring day, Keith walked the UGA campus in a gold
lamé jacket with a Mack Truck mirror hung around his neck and
his hair jacked out stiff from half a can of Aqua Net:

On that spring day, Keith wandered onto campus and met
Fred Schneider, setting in motion the series of meetings that
would result, after a few quick years, in the creation of The
B-52's, and after them the Athens music scene:

On that spring day, nineteen-year-old Keith strutted up to
the plaza, peered through his cat's-eye sunglasses, and saw nobody interesting. The band was awful. Nobody was dancing. Except some girl. And this guy. This guy in a tacky Hawaiian shirt.
That was Fred. "Oh, okay," Keith thought, "they look all right."
Keith was carrying a bag of pillow stuffing he'd picked out of a
dumpster he'd passed on the way through town to campus. Keith
didn't know Fred and the girl. He just thought they would get
into it. He danced up to them, stretched his painted lips into a
laugh, and shook above their heads a shower of shredded foam.

And so it began. . . .

2

FRED MEETS ORT — KEITH AND RICKY —
RICKY'S LITTLE SISTER CINDY — KATE COMES TO
TOWN — THEY ALL GET DRUNK AT A CHINESE
RESTAURANT — THEY START A BAND — THEY
GIVE IT A NAME: THE B-52'S

Would you like some Cheez Whiz?"

A pretty teen-aged boy grinned, cocked his hip, and held out the plastic tray covered with Ritz crackers and cans of aerosol cheese. It was Saturday night. A costume party. Bowie was cranked on the stereo and the boy was wearing his French maid outfit, the one he'd found at Potter's House and had altered to fit. Potter's House was the thrift store on Washington Street run by rehabilitating alcoholics where he shopped with his friends, all members of the confederacy of glitter kids out of whom would come The B-52's. He had dug for days through the racks and the rag room at Potter's to find the right dress for the party. So now, with his own cocktail set on the tray among the crackers, the pretty blond was doing a turn as Ruby the Upstairs Maid, sashaying coyly through the house, proffering his selection of tacky hors d'oeuvres to the dressed-up outrageous dancers, and not even waiting for their answers before choosing a cheese himself.

"Bacon and cheddar? Mmm! Good choice!" he said, as he squirted a loop of cheese onto a Ritz and watched it disappear into someone else's painted mouth, leaving crumbs stuck to smeared lipstick. He moved on, mincing in high heels through the sweating crowd as Bowie's "Aladdin Sane" rocked the house. It was just another weekend in mid-seventies Athens. The mid-seventies: a netherworld between Richard Nixon and Jimmy Carter: the downtime after Vietnam and Watergate, when the graduated and dropped-out student refugees from the sixties went back to the country and set up self-sufficient farms with a shotgun in the closet and a patch of pot in the nearby pine woods, listening to Pure Prairie League and the surefire narco-hit, the Grateful Dead.

While the nation rested, this group of kids in Athens refused to stop. They negated the slushy post-Vietnam retreat with glitter rock. They felt in tune with the creeping resurgence of androgyny. They *were* the creeping insurgence.

The party started at dark. Everybody was there—all the young dudes:

Keith Strickland wore his purple dress and similarly colored yak wig and eyeliner. Keith's best friend Ricky Wilson was there: Ricky, who, in his nurse's uniform, was even cuter than Ruby was in his maid's outfit. Fred Schneider was doing Ginger Grant from *Gilligan's Island.* Fred was in a gown split up to *here,* his lips painted blue. And on and on the house was filled with an assortment of students and vagabond androgynes in wigs and pancake makeup. If they weren't students, they were artists; if not artists, at least artistic, with their lives and bodies and the bodies of others being the objects of their studies and the material for their art.

The party rumbled to a hot pitch by midnight. By three A.M. only the diehards still stood. Feverish from dancing, drunk and antsy for something more to do in this boring southern town, they *vvvppped* Bowie off the stereo and charged out of the house to terrorize a 24-hour laundromat in the strip of businesses down the street from the party house at Five Points. They set off in single file, their cocktails in red-plastic, Georgia Bulldog, to-go cups.

They ran and skipped and as they went, Fred—excuse me, *Ginger*—faked a swoon.

"Oh!" he groaned in a breathy nasal falsetto Ginger-mimic as he crumpled to the sidewalk in his sequin gown and platinum wig.

"It must be the oxygen!"

Keith and Ricky picked him up and on they went, running, shrieking, spilling their drinks. As they crossed the street, the few cars out that late slammed on brakes in short sharp squeals as Fred, crossing last and running with little short Ginger steps, went into his faint in the middle of the crosswalk—"Oh! It must be the oxygen!"—and frat boys in their daddys' cars leaned from their windows and shouted "Hey, faggots!"

But the gang all felt strength in numbers. They all felt tough. They shouted back at the frats: "*Assholes!*"

Keith and Ricky kept picking up Fred, pulling him skidding and giggling until they got to the laundromat. Once there, these guerilla marauders from the party set to their freak. They screamed just to hear their own voices echo from the cinderblock walls. They did calesthenics on top of the washing machines and spun each other in the empty dryers. They jumped and danced to their own chants and frightened the few who were studying while they did their late-night wash.

Finally they all got bored and went home, when they ran out of mixers for their cocktails.

Fred Schneider always was a weird kid. He was seventeen in 1969 when he left his home in Monmouth County, New Jersey, to attend school at the University of Georgia. Like a lot of students, Fred never had any clear-cut plans for school and a career. He just wanted to get away from home. He picked the University

of Georgia because he heard the Forestry School was supposed
to be the best. He was interested in conservation ("Saving animals from extinction and that kind of stuff," he would later explain). He also thought it would be easier to get good grades at
a school in the South. He wasn't overly studious, but he definitely didn't want to go to Vietnam. When he got out of high
school he considered his options—Vietnam or Georgia. He didn't
think for long before he told his parents:

"I'm going to school!"

On his first day in Athens Fred saw he was in for a trip. He
was there for orientation, a day of hype about school tradition
and class schedules. The orientation leaders were all true
straights: ambitious sorority girls, geeky cardiganed guys. Fred
was unimpressed. But when he went for lunch to the dining hall,
Fred saw a long-haired, barrel-chested fellow standing up in the
middle of the tables and munching jello swill, a bohunk wearing
faded denim bib overalls cut at the knee and hemmed as shorts.

Big-boned and bass-voiced, the guy was shouting:

"Sterzings Tri-Some Potato Chips made by the Sterzing
Food Products Company of Burlington, Iowa, produce the finest
chip in the country, from the miracle state of Iowa!" He hollered
to everyone and no one in a mock whipsaw pinewoods accent:
" 'En I'd know, I've sampooled 'em awl!"

It was Ort—William Orten Carlton. Ort was a local boy just
out of his teens. Ort's face already sported a full beard topped
with black-framed geekoid glasses. His nose was red from rubbing. He wore blue sailor deck shoes tied with white laces. Usually, if he wasn't gripping some sheaf of scrap paper or bundle
of street trash while he talked, one of his hands would go into
the air to punctuate his hyperbole and recitation of trivia. The
other hand would find its way to the top of his head, there to
hover while his fingers curved like the tines of a weeding tool,
the middle digit digging through his oiled hair for some itch on
his scalp.

Fred Schneider was a goof himself, raised on too much bad

TV, a writer of silly poetry. So when he saw Ort doing the red-neck hillbilly cracker routine in the middle of the dining hall, he took to it. He stared. He thought to himself, "What on earth is this person doing?

"Whatever it is, *I like it.*"

Ort's voice blew through the dining hall like it would blow through the next ten years of Athens history: like the smell of boiling collards, funky and native. Ort was a character: large, scary, a bit uncontrollable, but never dangerous. He talked loudly and hugged strangers freely. He was a master of trivia and useless minutiae. To the kids who'd come to school, away from home for the first time and primed anyway for easy fright, Ort was a maniac.

"Hullo, Fats!" Ort bellowed to a skinny student sitting, now trembling, at a dining hall table. Ort held a styrofoam cup filled with the mixed crystals of instant coffee and white cane sugar. He ate it dry with a spoon and it stuck thick on the curled sucked hair in the corners of his mouth.

"Huh huh huh!" Ort donkey-laughed as he moved through the dining hall, an unofficial welcoming committee of one, inviting any kid who cared to join him in his bizarre freaked Athens underworld.

"Yes you, door-knob face! What are you looking at, *milk-breath?*"

Ort was a fixture in Athens. He was a native symbol, a standard. Like the Tree that Owns Itself and the double-barreled cannon, two Athens tourist attractions, Ort was something to be explained to strangers from out of state, new to town. When he was younger Ort had spent his late nights twisting the knobs on his transistor radio, picking up distant stations, logging the call letters in a spiral notebook. Now as he pushed past his twenties, he stomped through Athens in his tennis shoes and overalls or brogans and Bermuda shorts, scratching his head, pulling posters off telephone poles, scaring freshmen with his public excess, wrapping girls in his thick pale arms and boasting to them of his record collection. By the early seventies Ort's collection had topped twenty thousand items and he opened a record store downtown.

At the same time that Ort opened his record store, Fred was having trouble in the Forestry School. He hadn't anticipated that the program would demand chemistry and calculus, for which he had no love and at which he had no skill. He thought the program would be simply a sort of formalized sensitivity training in nature worship: how to identify trees and restore fallen birds to their nests. He also hadn't reckoned on being, as he says, the only hippie in forestry school—the only one in the school wearing bellbottoms.

Fred dropped out. Ort gave him a job. He made him clerk at Ort's Oldies, his record store. It was Ort who turned Fred into a record nut. Every couple of weeks Fred and Ort went on record-hunting expeditions to Atlanta. They ate donuts and drank black coffee on the sixty-mile ride to the city, and by the end of the day their blood-sugar levels roller-coastered and crashed. Their moods turned sour and they would scream at each other the whole way back.

Ort couldn't stand being cooped up indoors for any time longer than it took to sample the few obscure blue-label singles he'd find at the roadside thrift stores he regularly scavenged on his trips between Georgia and Florida, where his family had property. So he left Fred in charge. At Ort's Oldies, Fred penciled on a Little Richard mustache and played scratchy 45s on a wind-up pack-horse record player, while he and his friends hung out in the shop and hollered out the windows to their friends walking by in the street below.

Fred wasn't working one day when he went onto campus to see a band playing on the plaza outside of Memorial Hall. That was the day he wore that loud and stupid Hawaiian shirt. That was the day he danced to the band. That was the day Keith Strickland dumped the sack of pillow stuffing all over him.

■ ■ ■

Brown-haired and beatific, Keith Strickland was pretty. One of the prettiest in town, with smooth cheeks and tranquil eyes. He was born in Athens but his parents then moved to Comer, a small town twenty miles north of Athens in poultry country. It wasn't until Keith was in the ninth grade that his family moved back to Athens, where Mr. Strickland supervised the bus station, the cinderblock depot on Broad Street, just down the hill from the university's north campus, where the Trailways and Greyhound lines came through. On Keith's first day back to school at Athens High, the counselor brought him into chorus, his first class. That day was remembered for years to come as the day when the cutest boy in town came to school. Keith wore his favorite white bellbottoms. His hair hung over his ears, tantalizing. Keith walked in with his guidance counselor escort and all the kids in class, boys and girls, whispered, pointed, looked, gasped—and fell out of their chairs. "Oh God! Who is he?"

At Athens High, Keith met Ricky Wilson who was in the tenth grade, a year above Keith. Blond, shy and softspoken, Ricky too had grown up in Athens. Sweet? Boy, was he sweet. And cute? *Boy was he!* Before long he and Keith became inseparable friends. They had eclectic interests outside school: art, music, esoterica, a belief in extraterrestrials and flying saucers. For his sixteenth birthday, Ricky gave Keith a book on the Maharishi Mahesh Yogi (freshly famous from his association with the Beatles). They read the book together and practiced meditation. They reveled in the tripped-out absolute truths of the new pop guru.

During high school their musical collaboration began. Ricky learned to play guitar by watching an instructional program on public TV, picking out chords on a pawn-shop Silvertone six-string. All through high school he listened endlessly to Joni Mitchell and began composing songs of his own. In the summers Ricky worked at the local landfill on the edge of town. He saved his money and bought a two-track tape recorder. He wrote his songs, and got his parents and little sister Cindy to sing along.

Together with Owen Scott, another Athens kid, Keith and Ricky played in a rock band called Black Narcissus. For a high school Battle of the Bands contest, Black Narcissus entered and shook the gymnasium with a cacophonous set of Jimi Hendrix covers.

They lost.

This is the thing about a college town: The teen adventure isn't something on TV or in the magazines, it's right down the road in the rock-postered dorm rooms and the ramshackle rental houses. If you want to grow up fast and find the fashion edge, you can hang out with the college students and they'll show you how. The kids see the students around them—older, fashionable, with their young adult freedoms—and they like it. They get to imagining themselves involved in this adventure. And if the kid is cute enough, or has the proper sensibility, the bigger kids are themselves eager to let them play: "Come on. Hey you, sweetie, come here a minute. *What's your name?*"

Keith and Ricky liked hanging out with the older kids. And the older kids liked having them.

The hippest and the most beautiful of the older crowd was Jerry Ayers. He had a significant influence on Keith and Ricky.

Jerry had gone to high school in Athens. His father was a tenured professor of religion at the university. In the early seventies Jerry left Athens and moved to New York City. There, Jerry was a beauty-boy. He took up with the jet set, fell in with Andy Warhol's Factory crowd. Under his persona "Silva Thin," he wrote a column for *Interview*. He modeled tuxedos for French *Vogue*, and they say he flew on John and Yoko's wedding plane.

While Jerry was in New York, Keith and Ricky went for a visit. There they met the coterie of transvestites who did drag, and who showed them how to do it right—queens like Jackie Curtis, Holly Woodlawn. Keith and Ricky came back to Athens, reeling with the possibilities. That's when they started getting really creative. That was when they got the idea that even though they were living in a small Georgia town, remote from the centers of art and culture, world-class style was in their reach, just inside their mama's closets.

After high school Keith worked for his father at the bus station, saved money, and then together he and Ricky went to Greece, backpacking and living on the beach. They came back to Athens and Ricky continued at the university while Keith went back to work. One summer Ricky went to study in Germany for the summer and Keith went with him to hang out. Keith worked odd jobs, cleaning office buildings, washing dishes in the kitchen at a gray vacation resort on the dismal North Sea, while Ricky went to school.

After their return Ricky moved into a house with his little sister Cindy, who was working as a waitress at the cafeteria in a downtown department store.

Back in Athens after Europe, Keith and Ricky were writing songs. Owen Scott, who played with the two in Black Narcissus, was in another band with a preacher's son named Connor Tribble. The band, the Zambo Flirts, was popular locally. They played at the cafés and cowboy bars around town and, by all accounts, Tribble should have been famous. He was good-looking, charismatic, an energetic front man. He was a hero to the high school kids. But Tribble's problem was that he couldn't decide whether to shake it or stand still; couldn't decide on which side to flip his scarf. One day the drummer for the Flirts got busted for pot and they asked Keith to fill in. Although he preferred to play guitar, Keith agreed to play the drums.

After meeting on the plaza at Memorial Hall, Keith and Fred started hanging out together. Fred lived on Barrow Street, a short road down a dip between Barber and Pulaski Streets, in a run-down clapboard house under a water tower. It was a trash house. When a pot got dirty, Fred threw it out the window into his backyard. His bathroom floor fell in.

During those days, Keith and Fred would get together, smoke pot, and turn on the tape recorder. Fred recited poetry while Keith made noises, played his guitar, tapping the strings with hammers, slapping them with sticks. They called the project Bridge Mix. They had about ten songs. One was about a dog dyed dark green. A dog named Quiche Lorraine.

The dominant culture of the middle seventies held little attraction for Keith, Ricky, Fred, Jerry, and the handful of their wild-kid friends keening in the small-town piedmont-pine wilderness. They hung out around town, bored with it, fed up. To kill time and thrill themselves, they tried on thrift-store styles and album-cover attitudes as they pushed into their twenties. Even though it was a nice little town, their town, a playground, they wanted to shake it up a little bit. The way they did it was to dress up in drag and goof off in the streets.

At that time in Athens there was a small crowd of kids—the advanced, the intellectual front line—who were a transition from the hippies to punk/New Wave: they took Alice Cooper as inspiration and the New York Dolls as fashion advisors. All the boys, straight or gay, had at least one dress in their closets; all the girls had their Charlie Chaplin look. For those few years in the seventies, doing a flip-side drag was the way to express your independence. It was an *art* thing.

Most people ignored it when the pre-B-52's gang went around town in drag. The girls were obviously girls, no matter the suit jackets and baggy pants. But sometimes the frat boys, gullible by nature, didn't know the characters they scoped out and leered at were actually men. Fred had his mustache and ugly lips, and his drag was always intentionally dreadful and ghoulish. But Keith and Ricky were beautiful. At the Varsity, a local fast-food grease pit, they would be handed their mustard dogs and asked, "Anything else, ma'am?"

Like Fred, Kate Pierson had grown up in New Jersey. She met her future ex-husband, Brian Cokayne, a Britisher (Manchester) while traveling in Europe, and together they roamed hippie-free.

They never had any real reason to come to Georgia; Kate guessed she'd read too much Carson McCullers and Flannery O'Connor, gotten smitten too strong with the country dream. Whatever the reasons, they came south and settled on a farm they rented from the backlisted ads in the daily paper for fifteen dollars a month.

In 1973, the year Kate and her husband came to Athens, the surrounding counties were solidly settled with the old families who had pastured cattle there for generations. But in the given-up old farmhouses and reclaimed tenant shacks old hippies were scattered, their ponytails and madras midis snarled and tangled by wild rose vines, their heads filled with plans for building tipis and images of longhaired earth mamas panting through natural childbirth. In those years (last Nixon, first Ford) the woods slowly came alive with cannabis, a new cash bounty planted seasonally by country-boy outlaws who had faded into the fields to grow pot after the U.S. withdrew from Vietnam.

Kate and Brian liked their neighborhood. Up and down the Jefferson River Road their neighbors kept kitchen gardens. At their own farm they kept goats and chickens and grew crops of luscious tomatoes. On full-moon nights they often had their friends out for supper. They hauled tables into the pasture, and set them with candelabra. Their faces glowed with the light flickering from the antique stands. They drank homemade blackberry wine and danced in the field, while the cattle lowed and nodded their heads in time with the African pygmie folk music from the tape recorder.

After Kate fell in with the boho glitter crowd, they all killed days sitting for hours at the Western Sizzlin' drinking endless refills of iced tea. After an afternoon session of The Deadbeat Club (variously called The Oyster Club, Movie Club, Skate Club, Waitress Club) they drank beer, spent hours at Keith and Ricky's where they wiped makeup onto their faces, combed out their wigs, slipped into thrift-store dresses, and cruised the streets in someone's big car, looking for parties to crash.

They would go to Allen's, a dark and dusty bar in the Nor-

maltown section of Athens. Allen's was an institution, visited by
bikers, servicemen from the nearby Navy Supply School, and frat
boys. It had burlap on the walls, tacked with brittle and curling
travel posters advertising vacations in Europe and Las Vegas.
The wooden booths were rubbed and polished black by years of
denim- and motor oil-covered backsides squirming in the seats.
In a back room: pinball and shuffleboard. In the bathroom: an
inoperative rubber dispenser, the illustrated females long since
defaced by inked-in mustaches and disembodied genitalia seeking entry, the metal a montage of scrawls made by generations
of pissing men and boys, frustrated and beer-drunk and reduced
to clawing the enamel with pocket knives. In the booths out
front, the heroes of our story would sit and drink twenty-five-
cent beers, the men at the bar staring at the boys in wigs.
    The whole point was to go where they weren't invited. They
crashed parties where everyone stood around, guarded and tight-
assed. Kate kicked the chairs aside and they all danced on the
couches. They got into funny positions in the living room. They
straddled leg and hustle-humped stray thighs. As quickly as they
arrived, they left. They piled back in whoever's big sled they'd
hijacked for the night and careened across town to The Circus,
a local disco, where they hit the floor dizzy with tequila and the
readiness to challenge. At The Circus they got bottles thrown at
them when the boys tried to dance with other boys.
    When they weren't crashing parties they stayed home and
made their own fun. Once, Fred went over to Keith and Ricky's
on Pulaski Street and spontaneously staged a drag-show mimic
of Martha and the Vandellas, one of his favorite groups. Only in
Fred's version, it was Marva and the Marvelettes. Fred put on a
nappy wig and did Marva. Keith and Ricky wrapped their heads
in mammy cloths and were the Lettes. They did all the hits.

In 1975 a student entrepreneur and would-be culture maven
leased out a space at The Station, an old railroad depot on the
edge of town in which some businesses were located. He wanted

to make it an art house, but it didn't last long. He showed one movie, *Performance* starring Mick Jagger. But in its month-short life the place hosted the first tentative approach toward what would become the music scene. The guy scheduled a poetry-reading one night. He knew Fred, knew he goofed around with poetry, noise, music, and he asked him if he wanted to do something as an opening act for the scheduled poem-readers. Fred said sure.

Fred, Keith, Ricky, and some other friends wrote a few songs, gave them names like "Bush Hog" and "Dead Mink," rehearsed them, and at the show they played them all in an endless jam for hours. They crowded the stage area with any friend who wanted to scream, yell, and rock. They called it Nightsoil. There were three saxophones, a guitar, violin, shaking tin things, go-go dancers, a slide show of Canadian tourist attractions. Fred wore a shiny dress and had his lips painted blue. The audience just stared.

It was a lark, but everyone said the group should keep it up, work through the chaos, find the melody. But nothing happened.

By 1976 Fred wanted to leave Athens. He was entering his mid-twenties and still didn't know what he was going to do with his life. He knew something was going to turn up. He just didn't know what. But he did know one thing: He was sick of Athens. He left his set of odd jobs—busboy, waiter, dishwasher—and moved to Atlanta. While he lived there, he came back often to visit his friends. On one visit, that something happened which would change his life:

He and some friends got drunk at a Chinese restaurant.

Kate was there. Keith and Ricky, Cindy, Fred, and their friend Owen Scott.

After dinner and repeating rounds of flaming rum punch Kava Bowls, they went back to Owen Scott's house. Scott had been in high school bands with Ricky and Keith and in the Zambo Flirts, but now was in graduate school. Down in the basement were some instruments. They were all a little drunk and into fun, so they hung out in the basement. They started playing with the instruments. It turned out that whoever was there that night ended up in their new band. Except Owen. He stayed upstairs writing letters while they went to the basement and jammed on an idea for a song they called "Killer B's." After that night, Fred went back to Atlanta. But before he left they all agreed: Let's keep doing it.

They had all felt the desire to be in a band and had made many false starts before. Kate sang folk songs, Ricky made his tapes, Fred and Keith did Bridge Mix. Only Cindy didn't have any prolonged experience, but Ricky and the rest were convinced she should sing with them. She had been planning to go to Paris with Keith and Ricky, where they would sing in the subways, but then this new project started to work and they set aside their plans for busking across Europe. They all had material and whenever Fred came in from Atlanta they pieced together stuff and jammed. Unlike past efforts like the chaotic Nightsoil, their new project clicked. It looked so promising that soon after Christmas that year Fred moved back to Athens.

In February of 1977 some friends of theirs were going to have a Valentine's Day party. Fred asked them if their new little outfit could play. The party hosts said sure, hell yeah. The band rehearsed a few more times. A couple of days before the show, Keith came up with the name in a dream:

The B-52's.

THE B-52'S PLAY THEIR FIRST PARTY — FAKE FUR SHAG CARPET MUFF WIGS — THE B-52'S PLAY THEIR SECOND PARTY

Baxter Street is one of Athens' busiest strips. From east to west it runs through town from the low ground between two hills on the University of Georgia campus out to the edge of town, to just this side of the Middle Oconee River. From its origin in the great ravine where sprawls Sanford Stadium, the home turf of the Georgia Bulldogs and separator of the university's north and south campuses, Baxter Street rises to the top of a hill, dips, then intersects with Milledge Avenue, the town's main north-south street. Along that stretch of road stand the two high-rise dormitories: Russell Hall, home to a thousand boys, and Brumby Hall, home to a thousand girls. Near them, the more humble Mell-Lipscomb dorm complex, home to but a couple hundred of mixed sex. Conveniently situated in the middle of it all, halfway up Baxter Hill, is Bolton "Revoltin' " Hall, the university's main dining facility.

It was cold on the afternoon of February 14, 1977, as Keith

Bennett, a graphic design major from the middle-Georgia town of Macon, sat at one of the long formica-topped tables inside Bolton Hall. He wasn't eating—he had long since been put wise to that foolhardiness—rather, he was carrying out a more life-sustaining activity. He was making a list of the parties being held later that night. It was Valentine's Day, and as friends and folk passed by he picked up the party news. He noted, in what detail he could manage, the addresses of the parties, or at least their general directions. He tried to find out who else was going. He noted the themes, if any, since themes—pink, pajama, hat—were becoming popular party motifs. Most importantly, he noted the rumored number of beer kegs to be tapped.

It was standard procedure. Word went around campus during the day of what was happening later. Party news was picked up wherever it could be found: in hallways between classes, in the smoking room at the library shouted from table to table and overheard above the din of idle sorority girls crunching ice, begging homework off their friends. And what you heard you sorted, sifted, and doublechecked to find the coolest kick you could.

At the time, Athens parties were basically of two types—big or little.

Either:

A dozen guys in flannel shirts and Yucca boots standing around on a back porch of a house drinking beer from twelve-ounce plastic cups, draining fast a keg of Schlitz and talking shit, listening to The Grateful Dead and old Rolling Stones; smoking joints and waiting in teeth-gritting rough-house futility for stray good-smelling girls to show up.

Or:

Massive front-yard frat parties; multi-kegged, much-liquored, many-girled, hardy-guyed. At these, mostly staged at the glorious century-old frat houses along Milledge Avenue, the music tended toward Lynyrd Skynyrd, Steely Dan, Dixie Dregs, and novelty singles like "The Streak" and "The Monster Mash," repeatedly replayed and sung along to. Crowded, drunken, and usually open to anyone who happened by, the frat parties had an appeal just because of their enormity and the collective fevered insanity thereby engendered. At the same time they were heartily despised by the sensible and the cool because of the type of company to be found there: Greeks. So, the flip side to the massive frat party was the massive *independent* multi-kegged muchliquored, many-girled, hardy-guyed *non*-frat party.

These were all parties, sure, and they were easy to find. They were everywhere: easy liquor, easy crowd, much narcotic noise. But you had to work to find a really good party—a party that had that spark, that magic. And on that Valentine's Day afternoon, as the annual holiday of love promised rich party potential, Keith Bennett was working it.

By the time the sun was set, his list of parties filled a page.

That night, Bennett and his friends cruised the narrow, chilled streets of Athens searching for the fun with their third-hand directions. Schoolwork could wait. They followed the list and checked out the parties one by one. They drove by a few, counted the parked cars, looked in the dark yards for people they knew, checked the ratio of males to females, and guessed by the movements of the crowds whether there was still beer in the kegs. Nothing looked good. They grew discouraged. It was Valentine's Day and they couldn't find a decent party. They were getting pissed. It looked bad. All the other guys in the car were ready to give it up, ready to settle for killing a couple six-packs on somebody's back porch.

"But wait," Bennett said, "there's one last party on the list."

They drove to the corner of Milledge and Prince. Keith parked in the Dunkin' Donuts parking lot. He and his friends walked across the street to the party. The front door was blocked off, so they followed the gravel driveway around the side of the small clapboard house. They went to the back door. Once inside the crowded house they stopped still and stood. They didn't know what to do.

This wasn't their crowd at all!

In the living room was a gong and a set of beat up congas. There was a reel-to-reel tape recorder plugged into the wall and leaning against it was a four-string electric guitar. Barbie dolls hung from the ceiling and a guy was running around wearing a homemade T-shirt that said "The B-52's." Everybody was excited. Everybody was talking a little too fast and the music on the stereo was a little too loud.

This room looks like it's set up for a performance, Keith thought, but nobody plays live music at parties in Athens.

It was curious.

Keith Bennett had been to his share of Athens parties, but this one felt different. It wasn't a hippie party. It wasn't a frat party. It wasn't really small. It wasn't really big. He wandered through the mixed crowd and stared at the weird band setup until he finally said out loud to himself:

"What is this? What is this stuff?"

Then the band came out.

"Holy shit!" Keith shouted to his friends, unheard in the din of screams. "Who *are* these people?

On the campus of the University of Georgia in 1977 were fifteen thousand students with nothing but free time after class and spare change from their tuition checks. In a town so crowded with such kids there was no reason to notice these five who made up The B-52's. You might happen to notice Keith and Ricky walking down Broad Street in platform stacks with curlers in their hair. You might see Fred if you stopped by looking for old records at Ort's Oldies, or, now that he worked delivering meals for senior citizens, you might see him daily if you were over sixty-five. If you went into the Whirly Q luncheonette at the Kress department store on Clayton Street downtown, you might order a fried egg sandwich from Ricky's teenage little sister Cindy. If

you heard a rumbling Ford pickup truck pass by on Broad Street
while you were crossing, and, if you looked up at it, you might
see Kate standing in the back, her arms outstretched and draped
in chiffon, but then she would be gone quick down the road as
her husband, Brian, driving, grinning under a thick mustache,
gunned the old Chief and sped out of town toward their farm,
leaving a cloud-wisp of sparkling glitter that blew from Kate's
yard-long hair:
    You might see them all, but you would never think they'd
make a great rock-and-roll band.

That Valentine's Day night, the people jammed into the little
house across from the Taco Stand at the corner of Milledge and
Prince went crazy when The B-52's started playing. As Keith
Bennett stared, mouth agape, at this newly ignited frenzy, he
wasn't the only one wondering what was going on: Nobody had
seen anything like it before. Here was Athens' drag camp underground going public.
    The band had only just been named a few days earlier:
    After the first jam in Owen Scott's basement the previous
October, the group had continued to practice, but without a
name. At the time Keith Strickland, Ricky, Jerry Ayers, a high
school friend Tommy Adams, and another friend, Robert Waldrop (who would later write songs for the band), were having
strong dreams about female archetypes: Dark-haired women
came as hip-shifting succubi down the fashion runway through
their collective unconscious, inspiring their talk and informing
their drag. During the day they sat around the Western Sizzlin'
drinking iced tea, talking about the feminine visitations in their
sleep the night before; talking about what kind of costumes
they'd rigged from Potter's House party dresses for their nightly
cruise to The Circus, the discotheque down at The Station.
    A few nights after the band got the news that they were
going to play at the Valentine's party, Keith Strickland had his
own special dream:

"There was this lounge group," Keith says about the vision that tagged the band. "I had this dream of a lounge group and this woman with a big bouffant was playing the organ in this little club. It was just a vague little dream, and the group was called The B-52's. So I suggested that and everybody liked the sound of it so we said 'That's it!'"

They had a name.

"But then we thought, 'Oh no, everybody's going to think of bombers and destructive stuff like that.' But since we had always been going out and dressing up, I knew that B-52 was slang for bouffant hairdo, and I said, 'Well, maybe Kate and Cindy could wear bouffants or we could have a big banner with a woman with a bouffant put up behind us when we play.' We really wanted to stress that it's not the B-52 bomber. Although I did kind of like the connotations it had with the fifties. Sort of really Atomic Age."

Partly from concern about the group's image, but mostly from their already held habit of deranging their looks, Kate and Cindy added to their costume the night The B-52's debuted:

"Keith and I found the girls these fake sheepdog-fur pocketbooks and muffs downtown at the Diana Shop," Fred says. "So we told Kate and Cindy and they went and bought them. They each got a set and wore the muffs on their heads and that was their look."

"I was back there in one of the bedrooms the band was using as a dressing room," their friend Tommy Adams says. "They put on those platinum-blonde gorilla fur-like fake fur shag-carpet muff wigs that covered their entire heads and when they put them on it totally changed them. Then Kate said she had the shoulder bag that came with the muff but she couldn't use it. So I took the purse and put the chain up inside it and stuck that on my head and they said come on out and dance. And when I dance, I'm absolutely possessed. I can 'Dirty Dog' myself to hell! So I just started dancing. I danced from the first song to the last and that became a regular thing."

The year before, Fred had gone to a Halloween party as a hangover, with a broken cigarette hanging out of his mouth, wearing a T-shirt, a seersucker suit, and a painted-on pencil-line mustache. He figured that was a good look, so that night he recreated the outfit as he led the band with his chant-sing. Keith Strickland on congas wore a yak wig and Ricky Wilson wore a black-and-white striped shirt. Ricky also wore a straw hat with a shock of his blond hair falling into the four-strings of his guitar. He didn't look up the whole night while he and his made-up band played their irresistible rhythms.

The B-52's only had six songs in their set. They played their originals: "Killer B's," "Strobe Light," "Planet Claire," "Rock Lobster." Like they would do at all their early shows, the band started with Fred's walkie-talkie bleeps on "Planet Claire" and with ninety percent of the music prerecorded and played over Ricky's junkyard tape machine.

The crowd surged and danced. The Barbie dolls swung from the ceilings. The floor of the house bucked and buckled and threatened to collapse.

Keith Bennett was mightily impressed with the party he'd found and the people he met that night. Especially Cindy, the big-eyed, teenage saucy waif with the baby-doll accent. "She passed me a joint," he recalled years later after he had made her his wife. "But she doesn't remember."

The Valentine's party where The B-52's debuted caused a sensation. The next day, a buzz started circulating among the crowd of hip kids in and around the University of Georgia's art school.

Whoever missed the first show didn't miss the second when Theresa Randolph, who knew Keith and Ricky from Athens High, threw an engagement party for some friends of hers. Theresa, who as a child won a pageant and became the model for the blond Little Miss Sunbeam Bread girl, lived in what was called "the old Jewish country club," a lodge built in the twenties surrounded by a wall hedge of bamboo and pines in a quiet Athens neighborhood. It was two stories tall, with a sixty-foot party room and a fireplace man-high, big enough to walk into without bending. The second-floor windows opened onto the lodge's flat porch roof, which itself wrapped around the building. While the band set up that night for their second time playing, girls wearing recovered red silk and white satin party dresses strapped on roller skates and sped through the second floor hall, rolling out the windows onto the porch roof and around and back again.

The lodge filled.

As it filled and the night's darkness came on thicker, people at the party started talking louder. The invitational command for the party had been "Dress up!" so everybody was in some sort of wrap costume or who-am-I drag. Most everyone knew most everyone else and they all greeted each other in bundled bunches of hugs and hoots. They fell into piles on the floor, beer spilling. As new friends showed up, they all screamed in recognition.

That night was the first time Kate and Cindy wore their hair sprayed and laced up into bouffants of their own. The fake-fur muff wigs worn during the band's first performance had been a brilliant idea, and the thrift-store detritus look became their trademark style. The band was set up in the sixty-foot living room on a big Oriental rug. When they played it was pandemonium. People hung from the stairs and leaned in through the windows from outside. The girls on skates grabbed what strangers they chose for victim-initiates and hauled them into the bathrooms and under the running cold showers and then hauled them out again, now wet screaming skating through that darkly red-lit old Jewish country club, while those folk already very familiar or delectably newly met carried out in the shadowy corners of the lodge that classic Athenian agenda of innocent and magical illicit sex.

The only glitch for the band came during their new song "Devils in My Car," which was inspired by a radio preacher the band had heard while cruising. During the song, someone in the crowd tripped the extension chord. Most of the music was prerecorded, so the PA, the guitar, and the tape machine lost power, leaving only the congas and a gong. But nobody minded. They just screamed louder to overpower the silence.

Then all the lights went out, and everybody *really* loved *that*.

"Theresa was getting pretty wild," Kate Pierson recalls of The B-52's second public performance. "She was up on somebody's shoulders and was screaming, '*I can't believe this is happening in Athens, Georgia!*' "

MIKE GREEN GOES TO A PARTY — THE FANS, ATLANTA'S PREMIERE ART ROCK BAND — ATHENS STILL LATENT HIP

Mike Green leaned against a wall in the great room of that old Jewish country club and watched The B-52's play. He folded his skinny arms across his chest and cradled a plastic cup of warm beer in a crook close to his body to keep it from getting knocked and spilled by the dancing crowd.

So this is what everybody's been talking about, he thought to himself.

Mike had lived in Athens for a few years while attending the university, but he moved back to Atlanta in 1975. In Athens he had studied French and music composition on his own and took classes for fun until the school told him to stop, given that his transcript after nine quarters had become a perverse record of classes taken, ignored, and failed.

Mike didn't care. Never did. He had family money. After he was kicked out of school he moved back to his mom's house, and for the past two years before this eventful night had been playing keyboards in Atlanta's highly acclaimed, but scarcely popular, art-rock band The Fans.

Mike didn't know any of The B-52's personally; he knew them through friends who visited Atlanta regularly. In 1977, nobody spent the weekend in Athens. Not if they could help it. The longtime tradition was for students to leave town after class ended on Friday and head home to any of the towns anyplace through Georgia, wherever home was. Athens itself was nowhere. To stay in Athens was to be exiled, condemned to terminal boredom. Movies were slow to get there. Good books were hard to find. All there was in Athens, for the whitekid students, was frat rock, disco, and rednecks harassing anybody who didn't look like them, shouting (what else?) "Hey you, faggot!" The steak-house, one-mike acoustic clubs, and the bluesy southern rock beer-and-whiskey places presented Neil Young-slash-Joan Baez imitators or heavyset plaid-flannel and bearded, bluejeaned, hoot 'n' holler guitar rockers . . . and they all filled the clubs, sure, but that was only because there was no place else the kids could go.

Athens was still latent hip, like a secret yet to be discovered. Nobody really thought about the fact that they lived there. It didn't mean anything yet, other than that you were a college kid, which was not an insubstantial claim, sure. But it wasn't yet satisfying in itself to live in what was considered, in 1977, a cool-for-Georgia but still one-horse college town. Whenever anybody did think about the fact that they lived in Athens, they thought about how to get a ride out of it—a ride to Atlanta. Atlanta is only an hour away, down your choice of two-lane routes to the west, and if they could, after the last class at week's end, earlier if possible, the kids left their small nowheresville and headed out to the big city and its beckoning lights, both bright and dim.

On weekends Mike Green's friends from Athens went to Atlanta and hung out at what was called The Fans' house, where Mike lived and which doubled as a practice studio. And on one weekend one of those friends, Dana Downs, came to Atlanta with big news: Keith and Ricky and those boho glitter folk had started a band. Dana had lived in Atlanta the year before but had moved back to Athens to finish her degree in philosophy and psychology. She was hanging out with the art students, since the Philosophy Department on the university campus was located across the street from the Art School. The art students were a partying bunch and Dana was a party girl. As a child she was so hyperactive that her parents fed her sugar water and whiskey to calm her down. Dana lived with Theresa Randolph and they hung out with Keith and Ricky, since Theresa had gone to high school with them. On many nights Keith and Ricky went over to the girls' house with new records—Ramones, Patti Smith, Wire—and they all danced and did shots and got ready to go out, some slipping poppers into their pockets for use during later invasions of redneck bars.

Mike first heard about The B-52's from Dana when the band was still working up their set, cloistered and secretive in their sealed-laboratory phase. Mike missed The B-52's Valentine's debut, but he heard all about it afterward. So when Dana told him they were playing at Theresa Randolph's new house, he drove in from Atlanta to see what all the talk was about.

He stood on the edge of the madding crowd looking puzzled. Something definitely was happening. It was weird. He drained his cup and wondered if maybe it was just his own drunkenness that accounted for his amazed impression of the band.

Or were they really this good?

Ricky Wilson chopped at his guitar and swung his blond bangs from side to side in a syncopated rhythm with Keith on the congas. Kate and Cindy sang and warbled in their ticklish girl voices, contrasting neatly with Fred's resonating chanted recitation of their lyrics. The prerecorded rhythms were almost disco, and all together the whole thing was like a cartoon of a band. But it was working! It was all very simple, but the crowd loved it: They were dancing! It was nothing like Mike's band back in Atlanta. Nobody ever danced to The Fans. Mike stared out into the red-lit great room of the old Jewish country club and he began to feel uneasy.

As if to put into words the doubt Mike resisted admitting to himself, a friend came up to him—reeling, delirious, glazed from dancing—and hollered, "This is much more fun than The Fans!"

The guy was right. Mike knew it. He edged out of the room and went for another beer.

The Fans were the first big noise of new music in Georgia, and they had been regarded as the best of the progressive bands in Atlanta ever since Bruce Hampton's Hampton Grease Band broke up. That status was verified by their small audience. The fate of The Fans was in marked contrast to that of The B-52's.

The Fans had started in 1975, soon after Mike Green moved from Athens to live at his mother's house in College Park, a small-town suburb of Atlanta. One day Mike took the bus into the city to the public library. When he went to the checkout counter he set down his stack of records and books. The clerk, Alfredo Villar, was a recent philosophy graduate from Georgia State University, whose father had once been a highly placed scholar in Cuba before being exiled by Castro. As he processed the albums Alfredo noted they were all recordings of modern composers. He looked up at Mike who, skinny and pale with a long nose, seemed like the practitioner of some secret science, or the type of person who can be seen in cemeteries at night copying names off headstones. Alfredo and Mike began to talk about music, and Alfredo told Mike that he and a friend had a studio where they were working on an "electronic music project." He told him to come by.

A few days later Mike went over. He met Alfredo's friend Kevin Dunn and they sat around through the afternoon smoking cigarettes and talking about classical music. Alfredo and Kevin showed Mike their equipment. They worked over ideas for music projects in flourishes of grand theory. Once they tired of talking they played their tapes for Mike, and when he heard Kevin's guitar he realized that their "electronic music project" was really a rock band.

Alfredo and Kevin had been playing together since they were students at Georgia State University in downtown Atlanta. By Christmas of 1975 Mike had joined them. They found a drummer, Russ King, through an ad in the newspaper and they had a band. But they weren't going to just gig around. Mike, Kevin and Alfredo, blessed with more than their share of intellectual ambition and native capacity for theory, fancied themselves "maximally avant garde"; they used the phrase everyday. They were angry, combative intellectuals. Their music was their manifesto.

In the same formal way that they planned their music they set up ground rules for choosing a name: It had to be a common noun preceded by a definite article. They chose The Fans.

"Our name indicates the position we take in our music," Alfredo explained to a reporter for *The Atlanta Constitution* soon after they began to play out at local clubs like the Bistro and Bottom of the Barrel. "We are fans as opposed to stars, and our music speaks to the problems of fans instead of the problems of stars. . . . We are not a punk rock group. Our music is like 1970s British rock, like Roxy Music and Sparks. It is thickly textured. It doesn't have the dumb lyrics and crude instrumentation of punk. We're more polished."

In the spring of 1976 The Fans recorded a three-song single which they funded and distributed themselves. Alfredo's cousin Felipe Rodriguez helped pay for the recording. Mike put up money for the pressing. At the time there were many different formats for releasing independent records. After weeks of debate, The Fans decided they could get three songs on a 7" single if they recorded it at 33⅓ rpms. So that's what they did.

With that first effort their theorizing got the best of them. They recorded the single at 33⅓. But they forgot that jukeboxes spin at 45. They got their single on the jukebox at CBGB's, New York's hot new club, but when it played the band sounded like The Chipmunks singing Kafka.

Despite the embarrassment The Fans got booked at CBGB's as the opening act for another new band that had just put out their own first single, Talking Heads. In January of 1977 The Fans drove to New York and played. The next day they read the review in the paper.

It was everybody's dream: Go to New York, play a show, get a good review in the *Times* the next morning and read it over croissants and coffee. Partying at the Iroquois Hotel in a thirty-dollar room, the snow of a Manhattan winter falling outside the window, The Fans were convinced they were on their way, that they would soon be famous.

"Who cares if we never make money!" Kevin Dunn said, siding rhetorically with aesthetics over popular success, and wiping buttery croissant crumbs from his lips. "I just want to be the critics' darling!"

He should not have wished so hard.

Alfredo's cousin Felipe became The Fans' manager. How that happened, Mike and Kevin weren't really sure. Felipe's credentials, as far as they could figure, were that he had been a promoter of sorts for Genesis, Supertramp, and the Osmonds when they toured Brazil. And that he was Alfredo's cousin. It was Alfredo's band.

Felipe fancied himself glib. But when talking to the press he sounded like an open-shirted, gold-chained huckster. And such stuff made the cool kids wince.

"We are in an embryonic position right now in terms of contracts and the direction of the group," he told the *Atlanta Journal* from his office in Miami in 1977. "We are talking to labels, but I have them in a holding pattern right now because we are in no rush. The contract is there if we want it, but it should be the contract we want, something we feel comfortable with."

He told the reporter that The Fans had integrity. He said they wouldn't make changes just to get dates at clubs. "You can't manipulate them. It's been a long road, but they have stuck to their guns. It's like Alfredo says, 'The Fans, make it or break it.' "

When Mike read that in the newspaper, he rolled his eyes. " 'Like Alfredo says, make it or break it!' What a bunch of shit!" He had begun to doubt what he was doing as soon as he had seen the Talking Heads. When he saw them, The Fans seemed old-fashioned. And also, it simply wasn't fun anymore. He wasn't getting along with Alfredo, who didn't let Mike have any say in policy-making. Mike told Alfredo that if nothing happened soon, he would quit. Alfredo told him to sit tight, that a national recording deal was coming in a couple months. Mike figured he would wait it out and see what happened.

Then, that night at the party, while sipping warm beer, Mike saw The B-52's.

5

CURTIS KNAPP COMES TO ATHENS — THE B-52'S GO TO NEW YORK — DANNY BEARD RIDES ALONG

Any reason was sufficient but no reason was necessary for the folks in Athens to up and go to New York City, and during one of her many impetuous trips north Theresa Randolph, the one-time Little Miss Sunbeam and high school friend of Keith and Ricky, met Curtis Knapp. Knapp was in his early twenties, living in Manhattan, trying to become an illustrator. He hung out in the underground Manhattan scene and had been there during the early seventies when the poets like Jim Carroll and Patti Smith twisted their literary aspirations to fit rock and roll. Knapp was doing a little photography, some graphics, and had just finished painting a mural at Max's Kansas City, a venerable hip Manhattan club, when he met Theresa one weekend when The Fans played there.

Knapp saw The Fans and heard Kevin Dunn sing Brian Eno's "Baby's on Fire." He loved it. He met Theresa that same night. Double punch—The Fans and Theresa, *bam bam*—too cool. He

thought, "They're from *Georgia?*" He decided to go south. He followed Theresa to Athens. He figured he'd spend a quiet summer
there. Good place to get some painting done.

Once in town, he met the members of The B-52's. He saw
them play at Theresa's party and after the show he flipped out.
He freaked. He told the band that they had to go to New York.
"They'll love you up there!" he told them. But the B's never
thought they could be a part of the New York City club scene:
"Not us. Oh, come on! Curtis, you don't mean it."

But Knapp insisted.

"Really! You'll kill 'em. They'll love you!"

The band figured, "Okay, sure. *Why not?*"

One week in late summer, 1977, The Fans went again to New
York to play at CBGB's. Before they left Mike Green visited
some friends in Athens, and he saw Keith and Ricky on the
street. He told them now was a good time to come on up to New
York City and get themselves a gig! Keith and Ricky talked with
the rest of the band and decided to go. They drove north, eigh-
teen hours from Athens, to see if they could get a show. A friend
of theirs had shot some videotape of the band for a school project, so Ricky made some stills from that and sent them on ahead
as an improvised press kit. They brought along a demo tape.

From the beginning, they never had much hope.

In New York City they played the tape for the soundman
at CBGB's. At that time CBGB's was the coolest club for new
music. "Strobe Light" was the first song on the tape. The soundman listened to it and said, "I'm sorry, but I don't really see it.
You just don't quite have that ... umm ... umm ..." and he
went on about production technique, which baffled the band.
None of The B-52's were technicians. They'd recorded the demo
on the recorder Ricky bought working that summer at the dump.
They thought it sounded fine.

"You're just not ready for *See-Bee's,*" the soundman sniffed.
He played them a tape of The Shirts. "This is more like it."

Curtis Knapp was with The B-52's when they were in New York. He had come along to get some of his things out of storage because he had decided to extend his stay in Athens. Curtis liked Theresa. But he'd also found out there were many more girls in town just like her. Partybabes. Wildkids. So, with permanent red clay stains on his knees, he figured to stay in Georgia for a while. Get to know some of the folk. Get some painting done.

Knapp told The B's that since he had painted a mural at Max's Kansas City he could get someone there to listen to the tape. The B's left CBGB's and took the tape to Max's. They played it for the management. Max's was noncommittal, but at least the band wasn't refused outright.

They saw The Fans play. An okay show.

They drove back to Georgia.

Every day after that Knapp went to the bus station where Keith and Ricky worked and used the pay phone to call New York, bugging Max's to get The B-52's a date. He sat around with Keith and Ricky in the back of the bus station, hunched between the metal racks stacked with the taped and twine-tied packages, the roped-together suitcases. Outside, airbrakes hissed on mammoth fried-chicken puke-smelling Greyhound coaches. When the buses pulled into the little station feet shuffled slow on the linoleum floors as the passengers got in line. Ricky sold tickets. Keith loaded luggage. When at last the hard, wooden-church-pew bus station benches emptied and the buses rolled out, Curtis, Keith, and Ricky went back to gossiping about friends and talking about their band, Curtis working the pay phone.

Finally, after a week, The B-52's got a date in New York City: a Monday: the second week in December: showcase night at Max's Kansas City.

At the time that The B-52's got their first New York City gig they had only played two public parties. To warm up for the show at Max's Curtis Knapp set up another one, their third.

One day, Knapp went visiting some guys he had met: Curtis Crowe, who later became the drummer for Pylon, and his friend

Bill Tabor. They lived out the Atlanta Highway in a small house off the road, behind a gas station, down a long driveway, the yard filled with pecan trees. Knapp was out there and he thought the house was great. He loved the yard. He said, "Man, there's this great band, The B-52's, and you gotta get 'em to play out here." Curtis Crowe and Bill Tabor had never heard of them. But they agreed anyway. Sounded like fun. They said, "A live band? A party? Sure. *Why not?*"

So they did.

They bought a couple kegs. They moved the furniture out of the living room and into the yard and set up the drums on a big dining room table Curtis Crowe had made from scrap lumber. That party was the first time The B-52's played with a real drum kit.

Danny Beard saw The B-52's for the first time at that party. Danny had gone to school in Athens and graduated in 1974, moving back to Atlanta. In 1976, copping Ort's Oldies as an example, he and his partner Harry Demille started a used record store in Atlanta called Wax 'n' Facts. Danny hung out with The Fans, and he had helped them distribute their single earlier that summer. He heard about The B-52's, heard they were going to play, so that night he drove into Athens.

"They only had six songs," Danny Beard recalls. "The room where they played was smaller than a den and it was jammed. People were looking around the corner from the next room and staring in the windows. This was one week before their first show in New York. I got excited about it and sort of invited myself to go up with them. I asked them if they had somebody to do sound or to help carry equipment. They didn't have anybody so I did it."

The next week, the band packed up in Cindy and Ricky's parents' station wagon, which the band nicknamed Croton, and went to Max's. On stage there, a curtain hung between them and a jaded New York audience, only seventeen of whom had paid the three-dollar cover to see three bands play. The curtain came open and there were The B's: satin and wigs and toys and cute, and they started playing. They started with "Planet Claire," Fred doing the beeps on his walkie-talkie. The punks in the crowd just stood there amazed. What the hell is *this?!*

"Everybody was posing and sulking," Kate recalls of their first New York audience. "But our friends who came up with us broke loose on the dance floor and people just started dancing and all of a sudden there was a dance craze! From then on, everywhere we went, a friend of ours would get out there and start dancing and then everybody else would start. It was contagious."

Coming out of a scene of drag queens, reformed hippies, and practicing alcoholics in a small Georgia town, The B-52's were the antithesis of the hard raucous sound then dominant in the New York club scene. Where punk was political, The B's were absurd. Where punk was serious, rude, macho, and violent, The B's were polite, nonthreatening, feminine. The punks wore black; The B's wore thrift. Fred was a dapper dan and the girls were decked out in cocktail gowns and towering coifs. When a too-cool New York crowd stood around in the clubs, posing, leaning against the walls, The B-52's showed them it was all right to look silly; it was all right to dance. The punks mouthed off about being bored and mad at it all. But The B-52's said it was okay to be bored. All you have to do is find your mother's makeup kit and slippers with polyester pompoms, hawk a little spit to rejuvenate a dead eyebrow pencil, and your troubles are over.

The B's would steal fire from New York City, the Olympus of American culture, and bring it back to Athens, where they put the torch to the southern boogie and blues, drove it out of the clubs, and, back underground, triggered the next hip thing. The B-52's showed that if, as the punks said, there was no future, at least there was plenty of past to plunder.

Members of The Cramps were there that night and as The B's walked through the sparse crowd on their way out, lead singer Lux Interior stopped one of them and said:

"I have a new favorite band."

As they loaded out that night with seventeen dollars for their troubles (fifty-one total, split three ways) they were elated. *They'd played New York!* As they got ready to head back to Athens, Danny Beard, as an afterthought, said, "Did anybody ask if they'd like ya'll to come back?" They all looked at each other. "Nope."

Danny ran back inside and asked if they could get another date. The woman he asked opened her eyes wide and said, *"Of course!"*

When they got back to Athens after playing Max's, Cindy was excited because she'd finally got to see the Empire State Building. She was nineteen and had never been outside of Georgia except for one brief couple of months in high school when she ran away to Florida. Keith Bennett, that Macon boy who'd fallen for Cindy at the Valentine's party earlier that year and who was now her boyfriend, picked her up after the band got back.

Breathless, thrilled, sparking, all Cindy could say was, *"We played New York! We played New York!"*

6

JANUARY, 1978, THE SEX PISTOLS PLAY
ATLANTA — THE FIRST ATLANTA PUNK FESTIVAL
— THE B-52'S OUTPUNK ATLANTA

Her name was Doreen and they called her "The Rodeo Queen."
She worked at the Great Southeast Music Hall in Atlanta, just
helping out. She liked working there; the Music Hall brought
some great acts to town and she got to meet all the stars. That
was what she liked best about the job. Doreen was into that
country rock, and whenever there was a show she especially liked
she did the Rodeo Queen: wore a white shirt with fringe, tight
blue jeans, and high-heeled cowboy boots. She had a big felt
cowboy hat that lightly crowned her frosted shag. She looked
good in cowboy drag.

The Music Hall was a small venue set up in the angled corner of a shopping center in a space that had formerly served as
a Winn Dixie grocery store. It didn't get huge acts: max capacity
was only around five hundred. Through the mellow seventies the
Music Hall presented the standard fare: country, folk, modest
rock: nothing ever really too rowdy.

But then, in January of 1978, the Music Hall became the site for an historical moment: The Sex Pistols' first performance on American soil. Atlanta was originally fifth on The Sex Pistols' tour itinerary, but due to their criminal records their visas were denied. By the time Warner Bros. interceded the first set of dates had been canceled, making Atlanta the city the punks would burn first.

Stories of their aggressive behavior beat The Sex Pistols to America. For days before the band touched down Atlanta's newspapers were filled with reports of this outrageous new "punk rock." Parents were puzzled, preachers were disgusted, and editorialists indignant. They all railed against the band, that junky spawn of a decaying Britain, come to corrupt the kids into torn T-shirted nihilists, inspiring another wave of degenerate drug culture. The kids couldn't wait; any teen with delinquent tendencies and a taste for anti-intellectual anarchist melodrama was getting into the Pistols.

Rock-and-roll hedonism, combined with an ideological argument against conventional sanity, made punk appealing to a generation that had been prepubescent during the funfest of the sixties, watching with anticipation the antics of elder siblings but then ending up waylaid in their teens by the letdown of the seventies, when the human-potential romantic crooners like Jackson Browne, etc., were offered as the given. Despite how maligned they would become years later, in 1978 The Sex Pistols were new heroes. For the kids who never had a chance to riot, punk was perfect.

So on that night they debuted, Atlanta's mayor and council were on alert. The cops were called out in force.

When the staff of the Music Hall got the word that The Sex Pistols were coming, they got scared. They'd heard the stories: "The Sex Pistols, man, the ones who said 'fuck' on TV. Those guys who cut themselves and spit on the audience and thrash on stage and do that mutilation stuff, that safety-pin thing. Man, *fuck!*"

Usually, someone from the Music Hall escorted the visiting celebrities around town, took them to dinner, maybe showed them a little of Atlanta, did the southern hospitality routine on them, touring the Confederate zone at Stone Mountain, eating some barbeque. But nobody wanted anything to do with the fucking Sex Pistols, man.

Nobody but Doreen, the Rodeo Queen.

Doreen shepherded them around. They all turned out to be darlings. They ate prime rib at a local restaurant, sipping beers and only lightly gobbing on the scenery. Their one adventure was pulling Sid Vicious from one of south Atlanta's riskier housing projects where he had gone off alone to score junk, the white lady, heroin. She'd never seen crazies like this before, but Doreen succeeded in the end: She got them to the show on time.

It was a capacity crowd that night, January 5, at the old Winn Dixie. A local Atlanta band, Cruis-o-matic, opened for The Sex Pistols with an hour-long set of hammy, fast covers. (Johnny Hibbert, the vocalist for Cruis-o-matic, three years later would start his own record label, Hib-Tone, and put out R.E.M.'s first single.) At the show, while Hibbert and his band played a choppy, atonal New Wave Elvis medley, reporters scanned the crowd to see who was indulging in "the favorite punk pastimes of spitting and hurling of four-letter words." They noted in their reports the costumes of the crowd as though monitoring the spread of the disease. They found a few signs of the spreading pox: One girl wore a wrench hung from a wire around her neck. A guy had stuck a safety pin through his cheek. Another was wrapped in a homemade dress of plastic trash bags, cinched at the waist with a length of chain.

Press came from around the world to cover the show. So did the High Sheriff of Nashville, where The Sex Pistols were playing next. The authorities followed their movements with solemn alarm and fear. This punk rock was the harbinger of doom, the end of civilization as they knew it. It had to be contained. But the system did not crumble when The Sex Pistols played; there were no riots, no sudden flood of spit in the gutters. The effect was subtler: The next day at the University of Georgia Art School in Athens, it was all anybody talked about.

And Doreen, the Rodeo Queen, she rode that bronc. She held on. At the end of the ride, those few days while the Pistols were in town, she came down new. Like increasing numbers of kids that year, she saw the error of her current style and she felt the death of her cowboy daze. She changed her mind about herself and told her friends she was no longer the Rodeo Queen—it was over. She changed her blue jeans for black. She gave Johnny Rotten her cowboy hat.

Glen Allison, the manager of the hall, also knew a happening trend when he saw it. Immediately after The Sex Pistols played, Allison arranged for Atlanta to have a showcase of its own native "punk" bands and he organized a two-night lineup of whatever rock outfits then playing in Atlanta came close to the new sound. Allison himself got so caught up in the movement that he left town with The Sex Pistols to travel as Johnny Rotten's bodyguard. He was gone, off to abet the decline of Western Civilization. He missed the two-night First Annual Punk Rock Festival that took place a week later. He missed the moment when Athens superceded Atlanta and demonstrated its ascendance as the center of Southern Hip.

"You people have been deceived," The Fans' Alfredo Villar told the audience the first night of the Atlanta Punk Festival, Friday the 13th. "This ain't no punk festival." Nobody was really "punk" in Atlanta, not the kind of nihilistic dole-queue punk that went on in England; America didn't have a dole. Nobody could rightly figure out how to be punk in the South. A bartender at the Music Hall that night wore a torn shirt and wrapped a bicycle chain and lock around his neck, but he changed back into a polo shirt when the chain got too heavy. He hadn't realized that the hardware of punk could be such a burden.

The lineup that first night: Johnny Panic and Angelust opened; Cruis-o-matic played next, and did a punk cover of "Revolution" and a parody of "Anarchy in the UK." To close out the evening, The Fans strolled onstage with a cool hostile insouciance bred during their many trips to New York City. But the tension wasn't a pose. They really were seething. They had been together for three years and nothing was happening. They were angry. There were strains in the band. Introducing one song, Villar said, "This is called 'Dog Street' and it's not pleasant at all." They played their noise assault and drove the audience out of the hall and into the cold January night.

Snow in the South is special. Maybe once a year a light blanket will fall and stick for a day. And when it does everything is set off, highlighted by the unaccustomed whiteness and that particular sharp chill air that comes with the freeze. Every time it snows it is remembered for years, because everything seems to be unique fun then. Special things happen in the South when it snows.

That second night of the Atlanta Punk Festival, it snowed.

Despite the weather the Music Hall was filled. The Knobz opened, playing a speedy rock, concluding with their locally legendary "Disco Chainsaw," where the band chants as the lead singer grinds off his artificial leg with a gasoline-powered chainsaw. The Nasty Bucks, featuring future Georgia Satellites guitarist Dan Baird, played a set of raucous, violent fusion. Then The Fans again, the only band to play both nights, testimony to their status as the hippest "punk" band in Atlanta. That night they played a more melodic set including their cover of Johnny and the Hurricanes' "Telstar," which they put on their single.

Finally, to end the night, The B-52's came on.

Outside, the snow came down.

At the time the best-known musician in Athens was a guitarist named Randall Bramblett. After The B-52's played the Punk Festival, the Atlanta newspaper ran a story about Bramblett. He was from Jesup, Ga., had played with Gregg Allman, recorded two solo albums, and was playing with the Macon-based band Sea Level. He had recently settled in Athens and had moved into the old Jewish country club that Theresa Randolph had vacated. He explained to the newspaper why he preferred living in Athens:

"I mean, even in Macon you have to put up with that show-biz stuff," Bramblett explained, noting that Macon was the head-quarters of Capricorn Records, the label for many southern boogie bands. "But here [in Athens] the people are nice and friendly, and there are a lot of people just like me who I can party with and go drinking with and eat barbecue with. It's like a paradise."

Bramblett ended his interview with a foreboding request. "Listen," he told the reporter, "don't put anything about Athens in the paper. If everybody finds out what it's like, they'll want to move here and it'll get out of hand like Macon did. Let's just keep it the way it is."

Too late. With their Atlanta debut at the Punk Festival, The B-52's started the process that would quickly change the town:

Nicky Giannaris saw The B-52's for the first time that night at the punk festival. Nicky was from Atlanta but had gone for school to Athens in 1969, and he lived there for a few years in the early seventies when, if you didn't dress like a frat or a hippie, you were a fag and your life was cheap. Nicky had toyed around with bands since he was a teenager and lately then had been hanging out with The Fans. He heard about The B-52's and he imagined that with a name like that they must be a pretty mean bunch of rockers. But when he saw them that night he couldn't believe it. There they were, this bunch of "sissies and girls," and they were blowing everybody's shit away.

"It was the meanest thing I ever heard," Nicky remembers. "There was nothing like it. And in a matter of weeks, they sky-rocketed. I saw that something was going on and I hightailed it back to Athens."

Back in Athens Nicky got a job as a cook, rented a room for fifty dollars a month, and told his friends he wanted to start a band.

He told them to put the word out.

7

DANNY DOES THE B-52'S FIRST SINGLE — THE B-52'S PLAY THE GEORGIA THEATER — THE INCOMPARABLE PHYLLIS — THE TONE TONES, ATHENS' SECOND BAND

Danny Beard wore his trademark plaid, high-water flares and low-top Converse All-Stars as he watched from the back of the room when The B-52's played The Last Resort in Athens at the end of January 1978. The Last Resort was an old folk-rock cafe from the sixties on Clayton Street that had recently reopened as a club after serving for a time as a taxidermy shop. A few re-maindered heads still hung from the walls, moldy, moth-eaten, horn-chipped. It was The B-52's first time playing since the Punk Festival in Atlanta and it was their best show yet. Their timing was perfect. No long lulls between songs. Fred dominated as front man and the band kept it all together for two full sets. Kate and Cindy sang and danced and Fred handled his walkie-talkie and toy piano skillfully. They threw fish to the audience, many members of which had picked up on the band's image ("*Crazy! Really sixties!*") and raided the Potter's House thrift store earlier in the day for their own dress-up costumes of naugahyde miniskirts and polyester shirts. The show was simulcast over WUOG, the university radio station, and the phone lines there that night were lit with callers asking in disbelief if it wasn't all some kind of joke.

Danny knew it wasn't a joke. He'd seen them at Max's Kansas City that past December. He'd seen them at the Punk Festival in January. Now here they were at The Last Resort, and the crowd was loving it. Every time they played there was excitement, the buzz, everyone getting off on a real wonder fix that this local band was so hot. Danny was convinced they were onto something. He had helped The Fans with their first three-song single and had seen what they did right and what they did wrong. After the show at The Last Resort he had some advice he wanted to give the B's. They needed something to help take advantage of their momentum. He knew what they needed. Plus, he had a killer crush on Kate.

"Ya'll oughta make a record," he suggested after the show. "My treat."

The band agreed.

Danny put up the money and in February, at Stone Mountain Studios in Atlanta, they recorded "Rock Lobster," the band's most popular dance number, and "52 Girls," whose lyrics were written by Jerry Ayers, Keith and Ricky's early style mentor. At the end of the month Danny threw a party for the B's in Atlanta, at a room reserved at Emory University.

Demonstrating that punk and new wave had not yet neatly divided, *The Red and Black*, the University of Georgia's student newspaper, titled the concert review, "Punk Rock Plays Emory." "Rumors had been circulating that a virgin composition would debut," Kurt Wood reported, "but it was not to be. Fred Schneider (lead vocals) said afterwards that the band has been working on several new songs, but none had been rehearsed enough to play live."

The show was practice for their first trip back to New York since their debut. This trip they would play two nights at Max's and a Sunday night at CBGB's.

"Who knows," the article concluded, "the group may return

with a contract, in addition to further experiences in the North-
lands."

That spring, The B-52's traveled up and down the east coast between Athens and New York, playing CBGB's and Max's Kansas
City about once a month, coming back, not stopping anywhere
between, and riding back into Athens to glory in their little hometown, where they quickly became starlets. Kids from the university
began going to the El Dorado Restaurant to sit in its booths and
eat whole wheat biscuits and yellow grits, lingering slow over pots
of herbal tea hoping to catch Fred waiting tables in a bikini. The
kids in town were becoming aware of the new music do-it-yourself
movement. They began to feel, to see, that they, just these kids at
school, were a part of it. That Athens, just this town, this nowhere
Georgia hick college town, was where it's at. But even that still
didn't mean too much. Nobody really expected it to really work, to
really go somewhere. It was still small-time, underground, home-
grown—not yet noticed by the press. The B-52's were doing it
themselves, using what they had, piecing together a show that was
as much theater as it was rock and roll.

The B-52's came together when the hippie thing was giving way
to the New Wave thing. Fred especially represented a whole kind of
coolness about being clever and dapper and dressing up and having
a lot of clothes on. What is the opposite of a long-haired hippie lying
around smoking pot with his shirt off? A little guy with a bow-tie and
a little thin mustache doing wacky little skewed vaudevillian mono-
logues while Ricky replaced a broken string. The B-52's were harbin-
gers of a stylistic buttoning-down. The costume of the New Wave
wasn't hippie-style frayed blue jeans and oversized T-shirts. There
were no more flushed, nude teenagers. The new kids buttoned the
top button, hid their flesh, cropped their hair.

In Athens, The B-52's dropped the curtain on all the sloppy
southern blues. Their new stuff was choppy and non-sensual.
Hippie was about openness, softness, anthems and monumen-
tality. The new thing was about tightness and closure and snappy

tight songs: being bright, being quick, being ironic. In the dancing they got rid of the free-form, body-swaying style, preferring
the choppy, mechanomorphic moves of the pogo and the jerk.
The dancing was just as ecstatic as always, but was of a different
aesthetic. The B-52's hid and mocked their sexuality. In songs
such as "Strobe Light," where they metaphorize sex into a manipulation of fruits, they giggle about the nasty.

In May, when their single came out, The B-52's played at
The Georgia Theater, an old movie house with a stage on the
corner of Lumpkin and Clayton streets. It was their first show in
Athens since playing The Last Resort in February. With no clubs
in Athens willing to book a band of dragsters playing what was
mistakenly referred to in the street as punk rock, the B's had no
place in town to present their set. To warm up for another couple of shows in New York, and also to play for a man from Virgin
Records who was coming to town to court them, they organized
a show at The Georgia Theater.

It was a grand extravaganza. "The Incomparable Phyllis," a
waitress friend of Fred's from the El Dorado, opened the whole
show with a quirky performance piece that became a regular part
of the early B's shows.

Phyllis "The Incomparable Phyllis" Stapler remembers how
she ended up being transformed from nerdy art student waitress
to a little sub-starlet all her own:

"Really, I think what they needed was somebody to fill in the
show, to expand it, because they had to rent the theater and they
needed to fill up the time. They still didn't have a whole lot of songs
at that point. Fred and I were working together at the El Dorado, and
one day he said, 'Can you do anything? Have you ever performed?'
and I jokingly said I was on the drill team in high school and a few
days later he came back and said 'We talked about it and we want
you to do a drill team routine,' and I said, 'Oh, okay.' I had my drill
team boots from high school, and a friend and I looked through a
bunch of records and found 'These Boots Are Made for Walking.' I
opened the whole show. I came out to 'Boots' and just did a drill team

routine. I did it as straight as I could, with the stick-on grin they teach you, and kicked real high. And everyone loved it."

The Tone Tones opened for The B-52's that night at the Georgia Theater. The Tone Tones was the band Nicky Giannaris had formed after coming back to Athens, having seen the B's in January at the Punk Festival. Before the B's show he was practicing with Theresa Randolph, the B's friend, and Dana Downs, Theresa's roommate, Michael Johnson on keyboards, and David Gamble on drums. They called themselves The Responsibles. Then Theresa left to go to Jamaica and they changed the name to The Tone Tones. When the B's asked if they would open, they had only been practicing for a couple of months. Michael Johnson, the keyboardist, felt they weren't ready to play, but Nicky, whose band it was, was foaming at the mouth for the chance. Nicky said they fucking *were* going to play. Johnson quit and they got Vic Varney to play keyboards. Vic had never played keyboards before but he practiced for two weeks before the show and they played.

"After we finished the first song," Dana Downs remembers, "a roar came up from the audience. Well, that was *it*. Throw those college degrees to the wind! I was smitten. It was my first time on stage and I had found the place where I belonged."

The Tone Tones were the second band in the Athens music scene.

In June, The B-52's got an offer from Sire Records. Together with Danny Beard and a friend of theirs, Maureen McLaughlin, who had known Fred since 1972 when they were both volunteers on a student activities committee, the band decided to pass up the offer. They preferred to wait and write some more songs. They were getting more popular each time they played. They figured the contract offers weren't going to stop any time soon.

THE B-52'S ARE BLESSED — MIKE GREEN DISAPPEARS — THE FANS BLOW THEIR CHANCE — ATHENS DOMINATES

The B-52's' "Rock Lobster/52 Girls" single was selling. The band was loved. They were sometimes recognized on the streets of New York City, and were certain starlets in their own hometown. That spring of 1978, while they waited to take their pick of contract offers, The B-52's and their friends would drive around town. They would pass a bank clock and look and see as it turned its face to them, giving, after the temperature, spelled in light bulbs, the time. And it would be, like, 2:52!

"Ahhg!" they'd shout, and speed off, laughing.

Or they'd be cruising down the road in a big Cutlass Supreme heading out Jefferson River Road to Kate's farm in the country and they'd swing it over to a Majik Market for a six-pack. They'd send in, say, Keith Strickland, and when he came out they'd count their change, and it'd be, like, *fifty-two cents.*

"Yaah!" they'd scream, and peel out in a growl of red dirt and gravel dust. They'd rush to the river and all strip to the waist.

It was too much. It was cosmic. It was magical. Everything was falling into place for their band, and everywhere there were signs that what they were doing was touched and somehow blessed, full of grace.

In Atlanta, The Fans weren't feeling quite so optimistic. They were touched too, but with a curse. What little momentum they'd ever had was slipping away. They'd had a couple of singles and some good reviews, but no audience. It was Kevin Dunn's dream come true: They were making no money and they had no audience. They had become a critics' band.

Georgia-boy Jimmy Carter had been elected president two years earlier with his feelgood populism. The B-52's were being embraced because of their sense of fun, danceability, and anti-intellectual nonsense lyrics. The Fans' noise solos and assault art rock, no matter how aesthetic, no matter how solidly backed by theory, wasn't what people wanted.

Mike Green didn't want it anymore either. He couldn't work with Alfredo. He felt cut out of policy-making. When Mike made a suggestion, Alfredo told him to just follow the arrangements. Felipe, their manager, was on his nerves again, too. Mike felt a bad decision had been made the summer before when the band allegedly was offered a record deal but Felipe and Alfredo refused it. They'd wanted to hold out for bigger money. Wait for other offers. Let the companies bid each other up.

But no more offers came.

With no other companies showing interest in The Fans, Alfredo and Felipe went back to A & M, and they got the band a three-night date at the Whisky À-Go-Go in Los Angeles, the foremost showcase club where new bands play for record company geeks. Felipe told them it was a big show. Anticipating the trip, Kevin Dunn, with incurable optimism, told *The Red and Black,* "In five years I hope we'll be sipping daiquiris and reading stock reports, talking about how well aesthetics paid off."

Mike Green was skeptical. Felipe wasn't saying much about

the deal. He didn't let on too many details, and that only increased the tension among the band members. Then, when The Fans were getting ready to go to Los Angeles, Felipe said he was going to put a horsehair couch in a van and the band was going to drive to Miami to catch a flight to Los Angeles. Even though the record company was paying for everything, Felipe said that way was cheaper.

No one could figure it out. The record company was paying and Felipe wanted them to ride on a horsehair couch in an un-air-conditioned van to Miami, in one of the hottest months of the year? Mike didn't like that at all. Not only did he not like to fly in the first place, he saw no reason why they had to drive to Miami, sitting on a horsehair couch, to catch a plane.

Mike wanted out. He planned his exit for days.

At night he snuck his things out of The Fans' house where he lived, stashing them at his mom's. Finally, one week before The Fans were to leave for their big three-night showcase debut in Los Angeles, when The Fans were just a week away from sure fame, Mike disappeared from the scene and went into hiding.

Alfredo was furious. He angrily called all Mike's friends looking for him. Even when Mike finally returned a few days later, Alfredo refused to take him back. Dunn and the drummer Russ King watched helplessly as the horrible scene played out. They were powerless to convince Alfredo to change his mind and let Mike play the L.A. shows. Alfredo was adamant. He said they would get someone else. Although the posters for the show had already been released in L.A., Alfredo told Felipe to stall the record company.

"One month! Get us a month!"

He would find a replacement for Mike in a month.

Alfredo quickly recruited Tom Grey, an old friend who would later write the song "Money Changes Everything," which would be a hit for Cindy Lauper. Felipe got the band a delay, and they practiced until they felt Grey would work out. They felt they just might pull it off. When the time came they climbed willingly into the van, drove to Miami, and flew to Los Angeles.

But the record company was tired of the erratic Fans. Their original date had been scheduled at the prestigious Whisky À-Go-Go. After the delay the record company moved their show to a remote and unknown discotheque, where nobody was interested in what they were doing and where, when they set up for sound check, the sound man couldn't be found. Time came for them to go on and no record company people had shown up yet.

Which was for the better, they thought. The monitors were horrible. They couldn't hear each other. It was a cacophony. This was their showcase night and it was the worst they had ever played.

As they played with bad monitors and a ruined sound a rep from A & M walked in and stood briefly against the wall, assaying the band. After a few minutes, according to Dunn, he found Felipe, told him, "Felipe, I've got to tell you honestly. I despise the band. Good-bye."

Their chance was blown. They were crushed. They flew back to Miami. There, they crawled back into the borrowed van and drove home to Atlanta, silent, sweating, itching on the horsehair couch.

The contrast between the fate of The Fans and the success of The B-52's did not bode well for relations between the nascent music scenes of Athens and Atlanta.

"The B's just came out of the sky and got all this attention and the guys in Atlanta had been at it for years and they thought that they deserved more than them," Nicky Giannaris recalls of those heady first days when Athens established itself as the center for hip culture in Georgia. "The Atlanta music community had no grip on reality whatsoever. Someone needed to explain to them that pop music does not work on a seniority basis, like, 'It's my turn to get promoted now and be a star.' No way. It just doesn't work like that. I should know."

Feeling resentment, supporters of The Fans boycotted early B-52's shows and harbored a vicious resentment against Athens bands for years to come. They thought it was unjust that these naifs who weren't really musicians should be celebrated while hardworking avant-gardists should go neglected. They said, "They don't know how to play their instruments! They don't deserve it!" Atlanta's long-suffering musicians started referring to The B-52's as "those precious little bundles of talent."

Thus was born the first line of argument always leveled again and again, and always ineffectually, against Athens bands: *They don't even know how to play their instruments!*" But that criticism never mattered much. As if in reaction to that, it became almost a curse in Athens to have studied an instrument. Naiveté became a point of pride.

A split grew up between the town and the city:

Athens was quiet and pastoral; Atlanta cultivated office parks instead of flowers. Athens had ramshackle neighborhoods where it was safe and peaceful to run through the overgrown streets at night. The ramshackle neighborhoods in Atlanta were places of fear and crime. Athens was artful and chic, Atlanta wasn't. Athens had it all. Atlanta had nothing.

"Suddenly there was a strong attitude in Athens that they were all better than the folks in Atlanta," Kevin Dunn recalls. "There was a contrast. I think the Atlanta attitude just boiled down to 'Fuck 'em.' But of course that was spoken from a defensive and subordinate position."

Through 1978, Atlanta maintained a proud defiance. Bands still hacked it out, made tapes, and sought record company interest. But they just weren't cool. By the next year the evidence was overwhelming that Athens was the home of the best new bands. Atlanta soon began to pay court to that little hick town only sixty miles east.

"Until the total hegemony of the B's, it wasn't impossible to say we were a dance band," Kevin Dunn offered as a eulogy for The Fans, "although we had long undanceable stretches. We always had enough core Athenians who would come out and dance to us. But with the ascendency of the B's, we were consigned to the same category as the other Atlanta bands, that is, anathema for hipness.

"In 1977, we were definitely in the Top Ten of the hip. But just a year later we were on the ash heap of history as far as the Athens scene went."

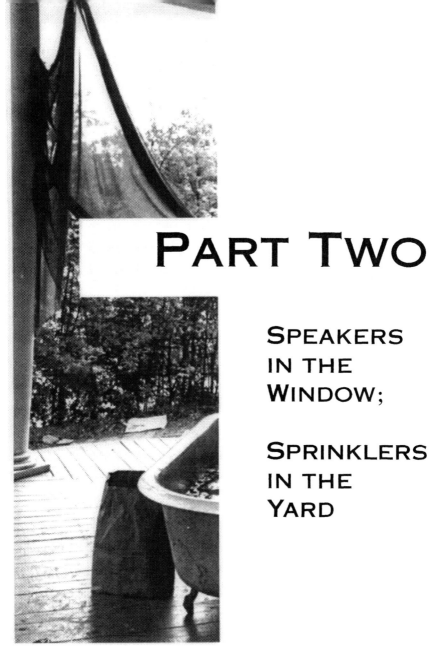

PART TWO

SPEAKERS IN THE WINDOW;

SPRINKLERS IN THE YARD

MICHAEL LACHOWSKI BLOODIES AN ARM — THE SCRAPES CLEAN DOWNTOWN — CURTIS CROWE GETS A LOFT — THE VERY FIRST 40 WATT CLUB

Having no theatre, opera-house, hypodrome, race course, or any of the fashionable city amusements, our young men are sometimes put to their trumps for some sort of amusement," noted an editorialist in the local Athens paper in 1860. The writer reported that the town was so lacking in diversions that a favorite pastime of the town's restive youth was catching a country dog, tying a rock-filled tin can to its "narrative," and letting it go, the pain on its tender part and the noise of hollering driving it down Broad Street, the main dirt road in town, while the boys along the street shouted some antebellum equivalent of the twentieth-century incantatory football chant, "Go Dogs." "The sport does not last long," the writer concluded. "But we are assured it is 'highly intellectual.' "

Nearly one hundred and twenty years later, the scene didn't look a whole lot better. To find diversion Michael Lachowski, who would in a short time become founder and bassist for Pylon, decided to start a gang. It was at a "24-hour party," billed to last that long, that was being thrown by Bob Croker, who taught art at the university. The kids in his classes, Lachowski a leader among them, often gathered at Croker's house out Cherokee Road, almost out to the country where the trailer parks begin. Any time was a good time and any reason a good reason for a party, and Croker threw his own on Michaelmas or the Feast of St. Crispin's Day, where the kids all drank beer while Croker read hilariously in Middle English from *The Canterbury Tales*. The art students and fellow travelers were the first fertile crowd for the new-music movement, and like precocious students always they hung out with their professors.

They liked Jim Herbert, another art teacher who was a favorite from the sixties when his old in-town house hosted naked hippie parties at which he filmed the lounging teen nudes. But Herbert had settled down since the sixties, and by 1978 the watchword at his house was "*Shhhhhh!*" So the art students carried on at Croker's, where, in the summer, they had dance parties. They put stereo speakers in the windows and ran through sprinklers in the yard, shooting each other with squirt guns until everyone was drunk and screaming and wet, dancing in the grass while they played the newly released 7″ singles: The Pretenders, Devo, The Residents.

It was just something to do.

So it was, again, just for something to do, that, at Croker's 24-hour party, short-haired and lanky Lachowski raised his plastic cup of warm Budweiser, hushed the room, and announced the formation of his gang. But he and his friends at the party weren't hoods; they were kids all with polite sweet intentions, whose idea of fun was drinking beer and lying during hot afternoons in plastic wading pools. They wanted to start a gang, but they wanted it to be a good gang.

In that summer of 1978 downtown Athens was a slow, small-town shopping district spreading a few blocks either way from the intersection of College Avenue and Broad Street, the center of town, where stood the university arch (the formal entrance to the university campus) and the town's obelisk monument to the dead Confederate soldiers. On that set of streets, more or less six lacing six, there were owner-operated dime stores and shoe repair shops, a J.C. Penney and a Davisons, a couple of restaurants, and a storefront run by Koreans where they sold wigs of straightened hair to Negro women.

That was the art students' turf: Many of them had studio spaces downtown. The university's Visual Arts building was only a couple of blocks away. Downtown was where they hung out before, between, after, and often, during, their classes: at the Wuxtry or Chapter Three, the used record stores that had opened up recently; or Helen's or Tony's restaurants, where you got a meat, three vegetables, and tea for $2.25, and you could count on the waitress to remember your name. She felt so familiar with the regular lunch crowd that she'd suck her teeth while she took your order and complain of her thyroid.

The new young art students flew kites in the side streets, the same ones where, a hundred years earlier, the kids of Athens had amused themselves by tying tin cans to the pink pegs of frightened dogs.

Downtown property was undervalued. Some of the storefronts were closed up. The windows of the empty buildings had become the town's bulletin boards. They were layered with old handbills, fliers, posters begging for the safe recovery of a lost dog, roommates to share a house, an audience for some acoustic act at a frat-boy beer hall. Variously pasted, taped, and glued to the windows, the posters were soaked by the rain, hardened and baked in the sun, until the layers made a crisp shell as hard as the plywood bolted over the broken front doors. There was little motivation for the landlords to keep their buildings clean, so these art students decided that they would do it. They called themselves The Scrapes, and declared it their mission to clean the old weathered posters off the windows of downtown buildings.

For initiation, skinny, red-faced, and boyish Lachowski picked up a fist-sized magnolia bud from Croker's yard and tried to scrape an arm with it, but it left no mark. He tossed it aside and picked up a pine cone. Lachowski didn't notice the wood-hard and needle-sharp spurs on the green cone, and so when he repeated the scrape he gouged deep and bloody tracks along the pale underarm of the gang's first initiate, who let out a yelp.

It was a bit more than Lachowski had intended, but with the first person bloodied the rest, all drunk and insensate, resolved to have themselves similarly scraped in all fairness to the unfortunate victim, who was hustled off to the bathroom to have his wounds slathered with Mercurochrome. Lachowski was the last to be initiated. When he got scraped he shouted, "Ouch! That hurt!"

"Hell yeah!" the rest shouted back in innocent vicious delirium. "Isn't it great?"

The gang then spent a whole day cleaning off the windows of a building on the corner downtown. They left one little square where they wrote, "This service provided by The Scrapes." Despite the Mercurochrome that had been applied after the ritual bloodletting, the arms of The Scrapes got infected. The scars were visible for years to come. That one downtown corner was the only thing The Scrapes ever cleaned. It was too much work. They didn't start any more gangs after that.

They settled for rock bands.

By fall of 1978 The B-52's were reaping rave reviews from the new music press in New York. "Another genius single of the month is The B-52's 'Rock Lobster/52 Girls,' " Glenn O'Brien wrote in *Interview*. "According to my calculations, The B-52s are the fastest-rising group in America today. This is not because they are from the South and unheard of, but because of a remarkable talent, which this self-produced single proves handily. . . . The B-52's are the most important rhythm band since, uh, Talking Heads."

The B-52's brought their clips of praise back to Athens, where a small crowd of kids who orbited loosely around the art school was turning on to the proximity of fame. The buzz and scene steamed during the summer as The B-52's single began to sell, and as the school year started that fall everyone with artistic tendencies put on a smarter face.

Athens was typical of many small American college towns, but the success of The B-52's bestowed a bewildering new sense of value to living there. Washing into town were the kids who saw in punk/New Wave their own revolutionary trend. These are the kids who came up in the early seventies, with nothing of their own and grownups telling them the sixties are over, finished. The general consensus was that the kids had screwed up their one chance, blown it. But punk/New Wave gave the kids of the late seventies the feeling that here, with the rip and rend of punk, was another opportunity. Here was their chance. As punk reached Georgia it drove through, and in Atlanta found black-leather adherents for its end-of-the-world angst. In Athens, however, punk was moderated by the rural air, its raucous sound softened by the plentiful trees and still streets. Then the B-52's came along, took punk on a picnic, and showed the local art kids how they could be rebellious yet still have fun. A crop was ready, and when the audience of eager students saw The B-52's succeeding, they said, "We, too, are of such stuff as they!"

With this awareness, the innocent isolation of the pre-B-52's bisexual bohemian glitter days was done; the formal Athens music scene had begun.

Each change of seasons brings changes in a college town. The University of Georgia is on the quarter system, so for three months at a stretch, nearly twenty thousand students between seventeen and twenty-three (the number grows slowly larger each year) occupy the town like a youthful army. As the quarters roll over from fall to winter to spring to summer to begin again anew in fall, the students are culled. Some stay. Some leave. Failures

are excused. The visionary and disillusioned look to the horizon
and head off down a highway far away from this backwater, with
their own secretly held great expectations in their sophomore
dropout hearts and a Jack Kerouac book tucked in the elastic of
their slip-on and easy-off shorts.

Leases expire and roommates are shuffled. Houses and
homes are emptied and filled again with different flesh as the
kids continually move, looking for cheaper rent, higher ceilings,
a more graceful space, a warmer niche. They move to be closer
to someone or farther away from another. Away from the ruins
of a love affair or the smell of a possum lost dead and rotting in
a wall.

Or they move for no reason at all.

That fall of 1978, Curtis Crowe and Bill Tabor moved out
of their small clapboard house in the country. They didn't have
to, but they chose to. They had lived there for a couple years
with two others, four childhood friends from Marietta, a small
town on the edge of fast-growing metro Atlanta. Their house was
out on the Atlanta Highway in a grove of pecan trees. When the
July and August heat beat them from the house they sat around
in the yard, shot skeet, drank beer, smoked dope. They loved
that place. It was a men's club. They had had some great parties
out there. And by that fall of 1978 the house had even suddenly
acquired historical value: It was where The B-52's played their
warm-up party before their first performance on showcase night
at Max's Kansas City the year before, the night they played on
the dining room table and that big girl Angel Dean sang a cap-
pella blues in the yard among the cars between sets.

Predictably, the school year had ended and the lives of
students everywhere experienced yet another of the periodic
shudders. A roommate at the house graduated and left. The vacancy presented Curtis and Bill with the task of finding a new
roommate. But they knew that no matter who they replaced their
friend with, it wouldn't be the same. They all felt that the tra-

dition of the house should end gracefully and not be dragged out by a sad effort to recapture the gone past with a new roommate.

They decided to move.

But they wanted to keep the lease.

Neither Curtis nor Bill really liked to work. They were always scamming for cash and they knew the house was good real estate. Together they reasoned they could move out and turn a profit by subletting the house room by room at a marked-up rate. They sat up one night with a case of beer and composed what they hoped would be the perfect ad for the house. They felt advantaged because Bill was an advertising major and Curtis had an innate sensitivity for the mechanics of a con. Their friends said they were crazy, nobody would pay what they were asking. But Curtis and Bill felt they had described the small but promising country house in such enticing language that they would have no problem finding tenants.

They told their scoffing friends, "Just wait."

The ad ran and the phone started ringing.

The response was so unexpected that Curtis and Bill ended up scamming themselves into a corner, the house rented before they were able to find a new home for themselves. They planned for a while to put a plank floor in a shed out back, but the thought of Georgia's wet cold winter dissuaded them, since no number of sheets of stapled plastic could seal the uninsulated walls and windows. They shivered to think.

Something would turn up, they were sure. But meanwhile one day that fall they were walking around downtown and they were bumming pretty badly. School was starting soon and they had to be out of the house. They strolled the sidewalk, rounded the corner where the silver-haired white man and his young black employee in tux shirt and tight black pants stood in front of their shoe store and beckoned women inside. Curtis and Bill turned onto College Avenue and were almost to Barnett's, the downtown newsstand, when they saw one of the storefront spaces thrown open. By nature curious, they peeked in. They saw a young man hustling bent and greasy, rigging the ovens and coolers for a sandwich shop he planned to open. Curtis and Bill were attracted by the excitement of such a work in progress.

Looking into the cavernous, empty first-floor space of a three-story building, and remembering that they were effectively homeless, Curtis and Bill flashed on an idea. Wandering in, they asked the guy about the upstairs.

"It's a wreck," he said. "Here are the keys. Take a look at it."

They took the keys and headed for the stairs.

"You guys entrepreneurs?" he called after them.

Curtis and Bill looked at each other, smirked, and then looked back at the sweating man, smiled, and said, "Yeah. That's it. That's exactly what we are. Uh, we're entrepreneurs."

On the second floor they saw that the guy was right. It was a wreck. Dust an inch thick on the floor and pigeon skeletons stuck with feathers. It was filthy, had tall ceilings, and was divided into small rooms by rough partitions. It hadn't been occupied in fifteen years. Trash was scattered and slung through holes in the walls.

The third floor was even better: the dust and silt even thicker and the pigeon skeletons more parched and ancient. Fourteen-foot ceilings, a giant empty loft space seventy-five feet long. Three tall arched windows at the end of the room overlooking the main block of College Avenue.

Bill and Curtis wanted it bad.

Turned out, the old man who owned the building was the uncle of a guy who did football predictions on the radio, so they easily tracked him down and after his first offer of seven hundred dollars they jigged him down to two hundred a month. Another scheme was already taking form in their minds. They signed the lease and set about finding art students to rent the spaces on the second floor. It didn't take long to fill them. On paper they figured if the art students paid their rent on time, which would be highly uncharacteristic of art students, they stood to make fifteen or twenty bucks a month on the space. And counting sixty bucks from the house in the country, they had a place to live and grocery money. They would become the Leisure Club, taking no jobs and living like kings in their reclaimed loft.

"Are ya'll gonna live here?" their friends asked, raising their eyebrows and scratching their noses when they saw the space. "Have you been breathing the air up here?" art professor Jim Herbert asked, appalled when he went up and saw the swirling final resting dust from decayed diseased pigeons and rats. He mouthed a twenty-dollar word from the Merck Manual, which he read for fun, and told Curtis and Bill they were as good as dead.

They persevered and spent that fall quarter hanging out, cleaning the place and rigging it with utilities, and securing it against the weather that would come in winter. They jacklegged everything. They jacklegged the plumbing: rigged a lavatory on the third floor with a stolen toilet. They jacklegged wiring: ended up relying mainly on an extension cord running downstairs. None of it was really dangerous, just not the way it should have been. It met code, if you squinted. By the time they'd finished their friends were asking, "Do you need a roommate?"

They had no idea that they were pioneering a new space in Athens in more than just the physical sense. They were settling the dark side of downtown. Doing so, they gave birth to the first premier party space for the nascent Athens music scene.

One night they gave it a name:

They were sitting around, disgusted and dirty. A stand-up lamp, two chairs, and a little table between them. The extension cord ran downstairs. A single bulb dangled overhead. After a long exhausted silence, Bill looked up and said, "This place is just about a goddam forty-watt club."

Curtis loved it so much he fell down laughing. "40 Watt Club" became their own private nickname for the place. By the time they got the place cleaned up it was Halloween. They figured they would have a party.

A week before the party Curtis and Bill tore out pictures from *Interview* and *Cosmopolitan* and photocopied them. In the talk bubbles they wrote, "I know where I'm going to be on Halloween, The 40 Watt Club." There were no directions, no nothing. They put them up all over town and word got around.

They bought a keg. Bought a couple cases of liquor. They persuaded some girlfriends of theirs to wear lingerie and mix drinks all night. As a party favor some friends rolled joints of bad Mexican pot and stuck them in balloons and hung them around the room.

To help recoup some costs Curtis had a friend handle the job of asking for contributions, as people climbed the stairs from the street below up to the party. He told his friend to make a sign asking for donations, because they weren't allowed to charge admission since they had no business license. When Curtis checked back later, he saw a sign posted above a desk: "Admission 2$, Geeks 3$." Curtis told him they weren't supposed to charge but the guy said, "Hey, don't worry. Watch!" When some people walked up he said to them, "You, two dollars. You, you're a geek, three dollars." Curtis watched, amazed. They paid it. He began to get an idea.

The room was packed. Everyone wore elaborate costumes, drinking drinks and liberating the joints from the balloons. That was the first night Curtis met Randy Bewley, another art student. Randy had bought this inflatable spaceman suit and carried a hair dryer and a hundred-foot extension cord to keep it inflated. He had a tube running from his mouth down his arm and out his finger and he went around sticking his finger in peoples' drinks, sucking them dry.

That night, Randy Bewley won the costume contest.

10

MICHAEL LACHOWSKI RENTS A STUDIO — RANDY AND MICHAEL BUY GUITARS — CURTIS PLAYS THE DRUMS — VANESSA SURE CAN SING — PYLON PLAYS

Randy Bewley was Michael Lachowski's best friend. They'd met in the dining hall on campus, but it was in Bob Croker's art classes that they became friends. Lachowski had come to Athens fresh out of Catholic school in Atlanta in 1974 and begun to take art classes immediately. He lived in the dormitories and hated it. When he met Randy, also from Atlanta, they talked about roommates and houses and getting out of the dorms. In 1977 they moved in together to a clapboard hovel on Barber Street.

By 1978 they'd heard about the new music that was going around: They went to the parties at Croker's house and were getting into the music thing. They didn't know The B-52's. They'd see them around, sure, but they were separate from the B's early gay crowd. Randy and Michael were part of the next set. The two crews might mix once in a while at an open party, but not much. Lachowski even left the party out at Curtis Crowe's on the highway when the B's played because they just really didn't wow him. He thought they took too long re-tuning between songs. They were a little too silly for his taste. A little too wacky. Too cluttered. He liked Kraftwerk. Man-machine music. Stuff like that.

Lachowski rented one of the studio spaces from Curtis and Bill and shared it with Vanessa Ellison. One day that fall he bought a bass at a yard sale and Bewley bought a guitar at a pawn shop. Excited, they went from house to house through Cobbham to tell their friends. "Hey, we're gonna start a band."

Nobody thought it was unusual that they attempted such a lark. They did it all. Bewley and Lachowski had the attitude that since they were already artists, they could take their canon of good taste and apply it to any form and do it successfully. They were already crossing disciplines by the time they bought their secondhand guitars: Randy, a painter, had entered a photography show with Polaroids Lachowski helped him mount, and won an honorable mention. Lachowski was a photography student, but when he entered a sculpture show with a piece done from black plastic, rubber hose, and lawn sprinklers, the juror, who was from up north, overlooked the other students' more traditional work done in wood, plastic, clay, and marble, and awarded the one-hundred-and-fifty-dollar first prize to Lachowski. Everybody got pissed that a non-sculpture student won a sculpture show, and that delightfully controversial reaction convinced the two that they could really do just about anything they wanted. They were hot. They were cool. There wasn't any competition.

Their successes convinced them that they did not need a lot of formal training to make art; the proper attitude and the right ideas were enough, and they could create work that was acknowledged at least as contemporary, even if it wasn't really any good. Their ideas were more important than technique. As The B-52's played and the new wave of bands and the revival of roots rock became the rallying point of the late-seventies student culture, Lachowski and Bewley figured they could do that music thing too. They subscribed to *New York Rocker* and they said, gosh, anybody can do this. They decided their goal was to go to New York and play once and get their picture in the *Rocker*. They could manage that. Sure. They set up a practice space in Lachowski's downtown studio that fall-into-winter, and with Lachowski playing from a bass guitar instruction book they hooked their instruments to a couple of pignose amps and started droning in tentative experiment toward what would within six months be Athens' premier resident dance party band: Pylon.

While they practiced, Curtis Crowe and Bill Tabor sat above them upstairs in their cavernous space monitoring the progress as the two guitars went on forever repeating three-note riffs.

"It was a cold-ass winter," Curtis Crowe remembers, "and Bill and I were holed up in the back of this ten-thousand-square-foot building with only about a hundred and fifty square feet heatable, and we would sit and huddle all winter long. We were both in school but doing dismally. I made two D's and an F that quarter and it was after that that Bill decided to quit school.

"Michael and Randy were rehearsing that winter and Bill and I would sit up around the heater all winter long smoking dope. Bill was taking this literature class, studying *King Lear*, but he's too damn lazy to read the book so he went to the library and checked out tapes for the blind. So we're sitting around this heater, huddling in this garret that's nasty as hell, pigeons flying around, listening to *King Lear* on the tape player, and in the meantime the primal strains of the beginnings of Pylon were coming through the floors.

"Bill and I would sit there and have scholarly discussions on how they were coming along. And we were trying to figure out what they needed. Bill said, 'These guys are really good, but all they play are hooks, nothing but hooks. A neverending series of hooks. No bridges or chorus, just hooks.' But I thought it was kind of good, and we decided that what they needed more than anything else was a drummer. And I was a drummer."

Curtis had learned to play the drums only the summer before when living out in his house on the highway after his roommate Charlie broke up with his girlfriend. It was a fairly serious breakup, and the other guys at the house indulged Charlie as he moped around for a few days. Breakups could be bad; let the guy drink, let him lay out of work, skip school. "He's been through hell," they said, "let him be." But he didn't get over it. And then he started playing dirges on his acoustic guitar, sulking in the living room, slowly strumming melancholy chords singing choke-voiced, "Oh, my baby left me. Oh, my baby's gone." Curtis and the other guys tried to be understanding, but it was driving them nuts.

At Christmastime 1977 Curtis went back to Marietta for the holidays. He ran into a friend who had some drums in his basement. Curtis bought them. For a hundred and twenty-five dollars he bought a bass, snare, and tom, layered with the lacquer and lumps of two dozen repaintings, now a glossy black, and he brought the drums back to the house, where his roommate Charlie was broken heart-unhealed and still stuck at half speed from his debilitating melancholia. Curtis knew something had to be done: He set up the drums and said to Charlie, "Okay buddy, here's the new beat," and he *slam* started *bam* blasting it out.

Curtis had never before really been a record buyer, but he started. His first purchase was The Sex Pistols. His current favorite was The Ramones. Then he started playing with some other buddies from Marietta in a band called Strictly American, but since they lived in different towns the band stumbled, crippled also by headstrong individuals and no leader or unity or direction. But when Curtis heard Randy and Michael playing, they had a definite direction, simple driving drones, pleasant and addictive like the hum of a favorite machine you work with everyday. There was definitely room there for a drummer with Curtis' style. Curtis was short and stocky. He could drum like a machine himself. But not the smooth tum-tum-tum of a rhythm box, but the jackhammer pounding of a steam-powered sledge.

"Curtis came down and said he would play a beat," Lachowski says about how Curtis came to join Pylon. "But he kept saying he was in another band and would only do it for fun. So Randy and I put up a poster for a drummer and Curtis saw the poster and said, 'What are you doing? I'm your drummer.' So after that he was committed."

To the three of them, the band was just an art experiment, another extension of art school. They called themselves Diagonal and they practiced through the winter. After a couple of months they decided to look for a singer.

They asked Sam Seawright. Sam was the lanky painter and brother to poet John, a notable character around town. They didn't ask Sam because he was a good singer—he wasn't. They assumed that since Sam was a good artist, known for his hallucinatory landscapes, *ipso facto* he would make a good front man for their band. But Sam didn't want to do it. Then they asked Neil MacArthur, another painting student. But when Neil tried out he didn't like the lyrics, and Michael, who had written most of them, didn't like the way he was singing them. Another no-go.

A practical joke led to a temporary breakthrough:

"I had made an arrangement with Sean Bourne," Lachowski remembers, "where I drilled a hole in the wall of his studio, which was next to mine, and he gave me the combination to his lock and I would play his records while I worked. So once when we were practicing, all of a sudden Sean puts on this record 'How to train your parrot to talk,' that just kept repeating 'Hello, how are you. Hello, how are you,' and we were going, 'Oh God! That's great, that's great!' We loved it. And so for a little while, since we were so into art concepts, we thought we would just use found vocal matter. So we had 'Hello, How Are You?' and 'Weather Radio,' where we would play over the Athens weather station, since I had a weather radio."

They liked the songs, but they realized that using found vocal matter would quickly become a gimmicky, constraining artifice. They still needed a singer. Then in February they decided to ask Vanessa Ellison—big-eyed, bobbed hair—who shared his studio. They all knew each other from art classes and from DuPont Textiles, a factory on the edge of town where Michael and Vanessa and a handful of other art students worked on the weekends. Vanessa had met and married Jimmy Ellison the year before and was living in a house across the river. Michael and Randy sometimes went over to Jimmy and Vanessa's house, played records, and danced in the kitchen. They knew she was a party girl.

"I used to go drinking with Randy and Michael, and Randy was kidding around asking me if I wanted to be in a band," Vanessa told *Boston Rock* in 1980. "One day when I was working at Penney's in the catalog department after Christmas, almost Valentine's Day, he came in. I worked not at the desk but at the phones in the back, and this girl I worked with came back and said, 'There's this real cute boy out front, and he wants to talk to you.' Like, nobody came in to work to talk to me. And I went out there, and he said, 'You wanna come down and audition for my band tonight?' "

"Michael was just really cool," remembers Vanessa, who herself met Lachowski and Bewley in one of Bob Croker's painting classes. "I thought he was so cool. Everything he did was cool. The way he dressed, the music he listened to, his art. He was in school but everybody looked at him like he was on the level of, like, a real artist. He was about twenty and just had some really neat ideas. He and Randy were both really bright."

When they asked her to audition for their band, Vanessa thought about it and figured that it might be fun. She wasn't exactly a singer, however. She'd sung in chorus in high school— alto, baritone, and a fake soprano. Her singing voice was always a little low and throaty for a girl, and a contrast to her talking voice, which was sweetly lilting and strongly accented from her childhood in the rural Georgia countryside around the small town of Dacula.

Vanessa came to her first practice on Valentine's Day and she brought the guys some candy. It was exactly one year since

The B-52's had debuted in public. When she showed up Curtis couldn't believe it. He hadn't met Vanessa before and here she was, this tall and big-boned yet striking girl, like a Weimar chanteuse with a round face and a country-bred wild streak. She was terminally shy and had little sense of rhythm. No one ever would have thought of a big girl like that as a figurehead for a rock band.

Lachowski wrote the words for their songs with a certain idea of how they should fit into the structure of the music. Everything was to fit on the beat, right in its place, consistent with the linear uniformity of the sound they were developing. But when Vanessa sang she stunned them all. Since she didn't have any idea of how to sing she came up with amazing weirdness. She cut words in half. Stretched single syllables for four lines. She didn't know what to do, so to compensate she attacked the songs in a fury.

Michael and Randy were into it immediately. Curtis had his reservations, but thought, well, it's going to be an interesting experiment.

Working at DuPont Textiles was an inspiration for Lachowski. Along with a handful of other art students Lachowski worked there on high-paying weekend shifts, and he was fascinated by the factory's clean order. Lachowski loved it. It wasn't mucky like the 1970s. It was ordered, unvarying, repetitious, like the music he and Randy and Curtis played.

After he graduated that summer of '78, Lachowski's parents told him they weren't going to give him any more money unless he moved back to Atlanta. Not wanting to leave Athens just when things were getting fun, he took the job at DuPont; Vic Varney had told him what a groovy gig it was, where he could make enough on a weekend to live free the rest of the week. To express how he felt about employment at DuPont, Lachowski wrote a song: "Working Is No Problem." Where some people felt that any kind of employment was a concession to The Man,

Lachowski saw DuPont giving them more dollars per hour than any other job in Athens. If you have a bad attitude, the shift will drag. But if you put up with it for sixteen hours on the weekend, you can live easy five days out of seven.

"It was great once I got used to working on weekends, which to me were sacred," Lachowski recalls. "At that time, being modern was really important. The seventies were so horrible, everything was bad. So we wanted to be the new arty, new thing, and the new music was perfect. We subscribed to the idea completely. I was fascinated with DuPont in a Kraftwerk way. If you didn't fight working in a factory you could look at it as a wonderland, with things painted neat colors. I was fascinated by industrial labeling, signage, and the safety image: safety glasses, safety shoes."

It was at DuPont that the band found its name. Safety cones were everywhere, marking boundaries, alerting workers to beware, to keep away, to follow the rules of order that were crucial to working safely in an industrial environment. In graphic rapture, Lachowski found the essence of his developing aesthetic in the shape, color, and function of the object. So when the band needed a name, having rejected The Diagonal as too pretentious, Lachowski suggested Pylon.

Nobody objected. So that was it.

Not three weeks after their first practice with Vanessa, Pylon debuted in public, opening for Nicky Giannaris' band The Tone Tones on March 9, 1979, at a party in the space above Chapter Three Records downtown on Broad Street. Nobody could believe that they had so many songs. When the B's debuted they'd had six; Pylon had a full dozen. Pylon didn't expect anybody to dance to them that first night. And nobody did.

11

The B-52's have manager trouble — they settle it — They sign a record deal — Their first album comes out

In the spring of 1979 The B-52's were the best unsigned New Wave band in America. Their single had sold ten thousand copies since its release the summer before, and had gotten extensive airplay on John Peel's national British radio show, which led to glowing raves about the band in *Melody Maker* and *New Musical Express*. It also attracted the attention of A & R representatives from the hipper independent and British-based labels such as Virgin, Sire, and Radar. The companies put in their bids but the band turned them down, waiting for a major label offer that would bring not only just good money but a committment to the band.

The B-52's told the press they were waiting for the best major-label offer. But that was only part of the reason for their delay in signing. The rest of the reason was that they simply didn't know what to do.

"They had no idea of the business," Danny Beard says.

"Most bands have a manager type in the band, but the B's were more democratic-like. They didn't have someone like that to start with. They weren't a well-run business but they had good instincts. I had some input."

For their first handful of shows The B-52's booked themselves, first helped along by various friends: Danny Beard, Theresa Randolph, Curtis Knapp. Ricky Wilson checked out a book from the local Athens library on how to read a contract and as they got offers they read the contracts and looked up phrases, and by the time they pieced sense out of the jargon they realized everyone was trying to rip them off.

During the initial rush of those first months as they rocketed out of Athens, Ricky made a list of scenarios, potential development: In three months have five more songs. In a year have a contract with a record label. This was the best they could do. Nobody knew what the record business was about; nobody knew what a manager was.

Slowly, however, Maureen McLaughlin stationed herself in the position called, as best anybody knew, manager. Maureen was a friend of Fred's from the University of Georgia. Maureen at least knew something about the law, having worked as a jury consultant on death penalty cases. More significant, she also had lived in New York City and knew the club owners, the musicians: Eno, Fripp . . . rumor had it she used to hang out with Patti Smith. She had an amazingly pure and high-pitched hick southern accent which New Yorkers found totally disarming and which belied her keen intelligence. She was the doyenne of downtown Manhattan, and her city friends there often got her to record their phone-machine messages.

The B-52's were on the verge of signing. But there was trouble in Eden as money inserted itself. For the first time the band was forced to reckon with that reality.

Keith Strickland remembers Maureen coming into the kitchen one day waving a contract in each hand, shouting in her high-pitched pull-string southern dollbaby voice, "Ya'll, I just don't know *what* to do!"

"Oh, no!" the band cried. *"Neither do we!"*

Fun time was over and it was time to get down to business. The B-52's faced their first tough decision as a band in the real world. Maureen knew something about managing, but it wasn't enough. It was turning out that Maureen, despite her social skills, was not prepared for the job. Tension and hard feeling bred as the band began to feel that Maureen was using them to enhance her own position in the New York City club scene.

The relationship between her and the band had never been formal. Maureen had organized their first tour in the spring of 1979, driving a Chevy van to Canada, Minneapolis, Ohio, and the northeast after the release of their single. But they needed professional help if they were to avoid getting ripped off in a record deal. They had been talking with Chris Frantz and Tina Weymouth from Talking Heads about what to do, and they suggested they meet their manager Gary Kurfurst.

"We met Gary in Washington, D.C., at a show at the Corcoran Gallery," Keith Strickland remembers. "Chris's brother's band The Urban Verbs opened and they brought Gary down to see both of us. Things started happening quickly after Gary saw us."

The band knew they had to do something. Gary offered to co-manage with Maureen, but Maureen refused and finally they had to fire her. That decision was the first sour note in their otherwise unfailingly bucolic and perfect adventure. It was the first recognition that it was serious business.

"It was a difficult split with Maureen," Keith says. "We really hated doing it. But it was a decision we felt we had to make. Gary was saying he would work with her if we wanted to do a split deal, but it was all getting crazy and we thought for the long run it was best to make a clean break. It was very emotional. Fred and I finally had to say, this is it. You could see it was going to get really complicated, so we thought we better do it while we still have the time. It was strange for a while, but later on I ran into her and it was agreeable."

Between firing Maureen and signing a management deal with Kurfurst The B-52's played Hurrah, a hip rock disco in New York City. The club filled to the limit and a crowd outside nearly rioted in frustration. Police were called.

"We really had no notion that so many people would show up at Hurrah," Kate told a reporter after the show. "I really felt sorry for the crowd. A fully equipped student film crew from New York University had added to the crowding, confusion, and disgruntlement of paying customers. We thought that it was gonna be just one guy in a corner and instead it turned out to be this whole crew."

"Yeah, we remember Hurrah," Fred said to Glenn O'Brien. "At that time we had no idea that our popularity had reached that peak. That was it, that was the night we realized something was really happening. Our dressing room was right above the entrance, at the door, and we looked out and saw all these people yelling. It really started all at once, after we got there. The monitors went off, and we were stuck on the stage. We couldn't get off, there were so many people. We just had to sit up there in the back, huddled in the dark recess."

With the deals all done, signed to Warner Bros. late that April, the B's faced their next tough decision: Should they move away from Athens. At that time there was no reason for them to stay. There were no clubs where they could play. The music scene was only then in its formative stages. The B-52's were too big for the town, and it was too expensive to keep traveling and playing in New York.

They decided to leave Athens and relocate north.

"See, we had a lot of things happen in the band when it looked like people were going to go their own way," Kate recalls, "but it would congeal again. Like, Fred said he was going to move to New York. But I didn't really want to move because I had such a great place. I was living the lifestyle I wanted. I really loved living there and I had a job I liked doing paste-up at the local newspaper. I couldn't afford to stop working, but there was some point I had to make the break. Then the paper changed my shift to the weekends, which made it really impossible to do both the job and the band, so I quit the job. I wasn't working so I was willing to move. If we could have kept living in Athens and done the band, I would have wanted to stay. But we felt like we were on the verge of something so we thought well, why not?"

They bought a house in upstate New York and moved in together. They recorded their first album in three weeks at Chris Blackwell's studio in the Bahamas.

In July 1979, The B-52's eponymously titled first album came out. A review in *Creem* was typical of the acclaim it received: "The B-52's are at the forefront of a move back toward the goofy, fun side of rock 'n' roll. . . . [A band] that almost unbelievably manages to hearken back to the early sixties dance craze era without sounding like a bunch of dreary-eyed nostalgoids painfully trying to resurrect the past. . . . They're so far out they're in. . . ."

After the release of their album they went to Britain. That's when the critics began to dive like pearl divers for political and social connotations in the concept of The B-52's, applying the politically informed tools of rock crit analysis to the way the B's presented themselves. Critics began to try to pin down The B-52's, but the target was elusive: They found traces of sixties revivalism, the Camp American Trash aesthetic, although they avoided noting its origin in gay culture. They cataloged their influences and the records they listened to: Amazonian marching music, Yma Sumac, African tribal chants, black girl groups, and Captain Beefheart.

"There wasn't any specific thing they all said we were trying to say," Kate said, "but they assumed that it had more serious meaning than just dressing up in some fanciful way."

Little did they know that it really didn't.

The band was very rehearsed. They were an act; it was per-

formance. Offstage the girls still dressed up, but not as elabo-
rately as the costumes for stage. Clean-shaven and dressed in
T-shirt and slacks, looking vaguely lost, Fred was mistaken for a
messenger boy by a rock writer at the Warner Bros. office in New
York. A British reviewer wrote, "They occupy the stage like people aware of what they're doing, swapping instruments smoothly,
concentrating deeply, suddenly jumping into spasms of demon-
stration dancing, a frug here, a slop there, some hully-gully everywhere. They neither let go of their straight faces nor seem to
recognise the audience all that much; at the end of each number
Fred will say something like, 'Thank you. This next tune is called
"Hero Worship." ' Then he'll return to the mike as if an afterthought just struck him and say, 'This is a dance tune.' "

For the time being critics ignored the lack of spontaneity,
or rather the fact that what looked spontaneous was in fact carefully rehearsed. They were temporarily won over by the novelty
of their rhythms, the freshness of their style, and their coy southern out-of-the-dark-of-the-wasteland new-discovery-from-the-
swamp oddball trailer-park Georgia charm. In interviews Cindy
was naturally saucy. Kate, New Jersey-born but with continental
experience, mimicked southern accents for interviewers and
never failed to tell about her goats back on the farm, milking
them, listening to the tough old rooster in the yard. Keith and
Ricky always mentioned their bus station resumés. Fred always
dropped that he had waited tables and delivered meals for old
folk.

And they won them over with their music.

"The B-52's play like no band you have ever heard before,"
a critic wrote. "Which doesn't mean that you can't identify the
moving parts; it just means that conceptually they are anything
but derivative. They embody a vision." The girls and Fred sing
like gospel call and response. "They are the one true new-age
dance band. You either understand rhythm and shape or you
don't, and the B-52's shudder with the stuff."

In another interview for *Creem* The B-52's repeat their wonderland success story. It's one of those stories that's so perfect everyone is dazed and tries to figure out what the secret was, what was the crux of it, what was the key, what was the cause, how did it happen, what was the secret sauce?

"*The Crawling Eye* was on the *Million Dollar Movie* twice a day for a week," Kate explained, "and we watched it every single time!"

12

KATHLEEN O'BRIEN MEETS BILL BERRY — THE STORY OF BILL AND MIKE — THE GIRLS IN THE SUBBASEMENT — THE SCENE HEATS UP

On the first day of May, 1979, the dark thrub chant of a Congolese mass sounded from a reel-to-reel in a room on the boys' side of the Reed Hall dormitory basement. Inside, the small room was jammed with campus-issue bunk beds, a metal dresser, desks, and dirty laundry. The industrial carpeting was hidden beneath a layer of books and records, and the corners of the room were beginning to softly turn blue with mold. Harlan Hale, a sophomore history major, stood on a stained over-stuffed chair and pulled a brittle-cured boa constrictor hide down from the steam pipe where it hung next to a belt of spent machine-gun ammo. Kathleen O'Brien, nineteen, smooth-skinned and full-lipped, stood in front of him, stripped to her bra.

"This'll be great!" Kathleen chirped in anticipation.

Kathleen was a DJ at WUOG, did a morning show, and she danced with the WUOGerz, an odd-lot band made up of students who worked at the campus radio station. When the WUOGerz performed, they packed the stage with any volunteers willing to go-go dance strapped in a straightjacket, or wear a wig and cat's-eye sunglasses, shake a tambourine or blow a discordant high school horn. The WUOGerz usually opened their set with a ka-zoo version of *Also Sprach Zarathustra* and then kicked into a set of New Wave covers and traditional rockers done punk-wise. The WUOGerz enjoyed minimal popularity, but despite their limits, and because of the efforts of their new drummer, they were scheduled to play a May Day concert with a popular new band called The Police, who were touring America on the strength of their hit "Roxanne." To get a show costume ready, Kathleen asked Harlan if she could borrow his snakeskin.

Harlan said sure. So that afternoon she'd come to get fitted. As Kathleen stood there, Harlan tucked the stiff ends of the long, dry, brown-patterned skin inside the wrapped folds and fastened the whole thing with finger-sized bobby pins and thumb-sized paper clips. Kathleen spun and bounced on her bare feet to see if the wrap would hold.

It did.

"Perfect!" she squealed.

A month earlier, the WUOGerz had found themselves in need of a drummer. Kathleen said she knew somebody: this guy named Bill Berry. She and Sandi Phipps, a friend who lived near Kathleen in the subbasement on the girls' side of the Reed Hall dormitory, had first noticed him one day when they picked up their mail at the little post office on the first floor of Reed. Bill, whippet-thin and with one thick, primeval eyebrow running across his forehead, lived on the fourth floor. Sandi thought, sure, he's cute, but Kathleen thought he was a fox. After spotting him she put the word out, and through the gossip circuit of mutual friends she discovered he was from the middle-Georgia city of Macon: played in high school bands there: played drums. So when the WUOGerz found themselves in need of a drummer, she suggested they ask Bill Berry, that foxy dude.

Bill, who in a matter of months would become the drummer for R.E.M., had only been in Athens since that January. He wanted to get back into playing music, so he was willing to try anything. When asked to drum, he agreed.

"Hell, yeah!" he said.

At the show, Kathleen wore the boa hide while she go-go danced. Bill borrowed a drum kit. During the show Bill couldn't take his eyes off that girl with the tawny body wrapped in a snakeskin clipped riskily with bobby pins. Kathleen knew it, so she shook special hard, and from her shaking great things would soon develop.

Bill Berry had moved with his family from Minnesota to Macon when he was fourteen. Before he left Minnesota his friends there gave him a "pity party," because they all knew for sure that Georgia was a horrible place to live.

One day in high school some friends of his were getting together to jam and they asked Bill to come over and play drums because the drummer who usually played with them couldn't come. He got directions to the house, went over, and set up. They didn't start right away because they were waiting for the bass player. Finally the bass player showed up: this skinny geek from high school that Bill had never really liked: Mike Mills.

"Him!" Mike said when he saw Bill.

"Him!" Bill said when he saw Mike.

After an exchange of icy stares and a riot of doubt they played, and the two soon became fast friends.

"We weren't friends at first," Mike Mills recalls, "because Bill ran with a rowdy crowd in high school and he didn't like me because I was a nerd and I didn't like him because he was an asshole, so it was a real shock on both our parts when we got together. But we gave it a try and have been best friends ever since."

Their band was called Shadowfax, after the horse of Gandalf the wizard in the *Lord of the Rings* trilogy. But their name wasn't as embarrassing as their repertoire of top forty cover songs and lame originals. Despite their handicap of a totally tactless approach, the band made three to four hundred dollars every other weekend.

These were the good years for Bill. He was making the money from the band, he had a part-time job at a junkyard, and he could fill up his Volkswagen for four bucks. He was rolling in money. Those were great times for Mike, too. He was playing music and studying hard, and was even picked as a STAR student, one with a top SAT score. But by their senior year Bill and Mike had decided in good conscience that they could no longer play Doobie Brothers covers.

"About eleventh grade, I put down the drumsticks 'cause the band Mike and I were playing with wasn't fun," Bill says. "We were doing boogie covers to make money. And that got old. You can do anything in the tenth and eleventh grade, but when you get a little older and you get that senior sensibility, you can't just play anything anymore. You say, 'Wait a minute, I can't play that shit.' So we all just bagged it. I didn't start playing drums again until the WUOGerz."

As the band was breaking up Bill got the break that would eventually make him a seriously happy man: He got a job at Paragon, the booking agency for Capricorn Records, the label that grew fat from the 1970s popularity of Southern Rock acts like the Allman Brothers and Wet Willie.

It was a job he lucked into:

"Get this," Bill says. "Our guitarist's girlfriend's brother had this job at Paragon, and a friend of his was trying out for the police force. So this guy who had the job went with his friend to take the tests to see if you're capable of being a cop. I don't know why he took the tests, too. Just to do it, I think. But anyway, he passed the test and for some reason he became a cop. It was just the weirdest thing. He had this great job at Paragon, but he couldn't keep it since he was going to become a cop, so he said to me he said, 'You want the job?' And I said, '*Fuck!*'

"I couldn't believe it. Anybody would take that job: picking up rock stars at the Atlanta airport. I met a lot of people that way and during the day had menial work to do, mailing and stuff. So I had forty hours during the day and then after work all this extra stuff like picking up rock stars was overtime. But I would have paid to do it. Here's this eighteen-year-old kid who got double-time to go spend the night out with rock stars. Plus, I could snitch bottles of liquor out of the limousines. It was great!"

At Paragon, Bill met Ian Copeland. Copeland had come from England to work for Paragon and he'd brought with him his own stable of bands he wanted to break in America, like The Buzzcocks and The Police, which featured his brother Stewart. Through Copeland, Bill and Mike's interest in playing music was revived.

"We'd both gotten disenchanted with music until Ian started playing The Damned and Chelsea and The Ramones. Without Ian, you wouldn't have known about that stuff in Macon," says Mike.

"Ian turned me on to Richard Hell, The Sex Pistols, all this shit," Bill says. "He became an instant hero to me and I clung to him among the other agents. I lived next door practically, so when he worked late I would hang out in his office and listen while he was cutting deals over the phone. I was trying to learn what I could about the business."

In the fall of 1978 Bill and Mike were living in an apartment together. Bill worked at Paragon. Mike worked at Sears. One night they were on their way to a Mexican restaurant and they stopped in a K-mart parking lot and Mike called his dad to tell him what they were doing. The phone call triggered something that would change both their lives. Mike got on the phone and, out of the blue, his dad, Frank, started yelling at Mike about how here he was a STAR student, highest SAT in the class, and he was working at Sears and for all intents and good guesses was being profligate with his birthright of a keen intelligence. Mike was dumbfounded.

Mike came back to the car and said, "I can't believe it. My dad just jumped into my shit."

Over dinner, Bill and Mike talked about leaving Macon. Talked about going to school or something, just get the hell out. By the time they'd finished slopping up the bean juice from their burritos, they decided to head to Athens, off to the University of Georgia.

Since they made their decision to go to school so late in the year, they waited until winter quarter to enter. Mike had, more or less, decided upon journalism as his major. Bill, though, had a more definite plan. His idea was to get a law degree or an MBA and go into managing sports figures, or artists in the music business. At Paragon Bill had met John Huie, a college rep for the company, and Huie told Bill that when he got to Athens he should look up an old friend of his from his undergraduate days at Davison College: a law student named Bertis Downs, who was working on the university's concert committee. Bill said he'd do it.

So in January 1979 the two best friends from Macon moved to Athens. Mike moved into Myers Hall. Bill moved into Reed. In Reed Hall, Bill discovered a new world.

In hindsight it all seems like too much to be a coincidence, and it will indeed come to be remarked on frequently in the later years, after the establishment of the Athens rock-and-roll empire, and pointed to as evidence that the coming together of the scene then, in those last few years of the seventies, was something greater than simple happenstance and was instead inspired by some palpable mad magic: During the school year 1978-1979, not only did Curtis Crowe move into the loft space on College Avenue that inspired the 40 Watt Club and lease a studio to Michael Lachowski, thereby midwifing Pylon, "The greatest Athens dance band," but, that same schoolyear as R.E.M.'s drummer-to-be Bill Berry moved onto the fourth floor, a crucial vanguard of the first generation moved to Athens and, with bedsprings, blotter acid, and black eye makeup, cobbled according to instructions of their own instinctive devising a crucible of decadence in the subbasement of the university's Reed Hall dormitory.

Reed Hall stands as part of a dorm complex halfway down the sloping geography from the old campus, at the top of the town's hill-set, to the deep between-hill trough where sits Sanford Stadium. Reed is four stories and a basement, divided down the middle by two sets of fireproof doors: half for boys, half for girls. But Reed was built on a hill, and on one side, there on the slope side of the crest, there was below the basement level space yet again for a partial hall, for years left to be the furnace space but that lately the housing-short campus authority had roomed off and outfitted with bunk beds and metal dressers. Assigned two to a room in the set of ten, the subbasement was home to twenty young women. Being so few, the campus housing authority did not assign a hall monitor to live on the floor and so the girls were left to be the responsibility of the devout Catholic "resident assistant" on the basement level; for all practical purposes, they were unsupervised. "Surely we can trust them to behave," some decision-maker had said. "They're only girls, after all."

Mistake.

Reed was the dorm closest to Sanford Stadium. During football season Sanford Stadium became sacred ground, the place where tens of thousands gathered and for the weekend changed the face of Athens from a sleepy student town to a place of festival and rampage. On home game days in the fall, those fans faithful to the Georgia Bulldog football team caravaned into Athens, driving Winnebagos, Lincoln Towncars, or pickups, all with horns that played a variation on Dixie. Since Reed Hall lay in the middle of the shortest route between downtown parking and the football stadium, on those chaotic fall Saturdays the unlucky residents of Reed with ground-floor room assignments were forced to suffer those Bulldog fans, as they, the game-goers, trudged laughing across campus with bellies full of beer and the grease of fried chicken still on their fingers from their ritual pre-game tailgate picnics. Alumni from across Georgia, used-car

salesmen and their pouch-bellied wives in red and black stretch
pants shuffled by the windows of the dorm rooms on crepe-soled
sensible shoes. Neat and necktied frat boys passed, talking po-
litely of intramural politics or the latest softball scandal, while on
each arm they escorted cute girls for dates who had flasks of
Coca-Cola and bourbon hidden in their purses next to their di-
aphragm cases. (During a game it was not unusual for the still-
ness of the Reed Hall parking lot to be broken by the convulsive
drunken stumbling of one of those same coy sweet wide-mouthed
southern sorority girls, led from the stadium stands by her be-
grudging boyfriend and allowed to wretch discretely in the hedge
of applejack and redtip that surrounded the dorm.) To and from
the stadium pimpled redneck boys in baseball caps roughhoused
and wrestled their way past the dorm room windows in sweaty
heaps of five and six, barking back and forth in solidarity with
the team "Woof! woof! woof!" and irritating to no end the girls
in the subbasement who *hated* football.

Mostly Catholics and Episcopalians from Atlanta, the girls
assigned down there proved a volatile mix. Something sparked,
and just a week after classes started that fall the "subwastement"
became one of the centers of the storm system that makes up a
college campus when staffed in full complement with hordes of
teenagers in full estrus and rut.

The girls moved into the subbasement in the fall, set up their
stereos, and began the weaving of introductions and meetings that
would lead them out from their dormitory cells up the hill into the
town itself, like a lost tribe finding itself saved and rescued, pulled
out of normal collegiate desolation by hand-to-hand party meetings,
up and out and into the heart of a coming scene in a great chain of
begettings that created a community out of a roughshaken set of
strangers, friends and friends of friends.

This is how it happened:

Linda Hopper, who would later become the singer for a crit-
ically acclaimed Athens band called Oh-OK, lived in Athens in
1977, but she didn't count that year because she hadn't known

anybody and had absolutely the worst time possible. The summer before the new school year started in September 1978 Linda talked her high school friend Sandi Phipps into transferring from Kennesaw College in Atlanta to the University of Georgia in Athens. Linda told Sandi to ask for Reed Hall because that's what she was asking for. So Sandi did it. But that fall Linda decided to wait until winter quarter to start back, and eighteen-year-old Sandi, who would set up R.E.M.'s first corporate office and later be voted a Top 10 rock photographer by the readers of *Creem* magazine, was assigned to Reed Hall, the subbasement, and she moved in that fall not knowing a soul.

While Sandi was blond with green, almond-angled eyes and matching slashing cheekbones, Kathy Russo was sultry dark Italian. They each moved with a bounce on their small feet and still fit their Girl Scout uniforms. Kathy was assigned the room next to Sandi's in the subbasement and they met when Kathy saw Sandi in the hallway. Kathy said to Sandi, "Hey, let's go get stoned."

There, in Kathy's room, Sandi met Carol Levy, a self-styled "misplaced Joan of Arc" with her black hair cut in an aggressive Patti Smith shag. Carol would play in the band Boat Of, shoot R.E.M.'s first publicity photos, and inspire Michael Stipe to greatness. When Sandi walked into the room, Carol, who lived on the fourth floor of Reed, grinned a vicious leer and, already speaking perfect punk, greeted Sandi with a studied attitude.

"Who the *fuck* are you?"

Down in the subbasement, rock ruled. Kathleen O'Brien, who would later make the crucial introductions that would lead to the formation of R.E.M., grew pot on her bottom bunk after her roommate dropped out; her botany teacher gave her the seeds for an experiment in phototropism. Sandi and Kathy were taking the highly touted course in the history department on Maoism, and while they struggled in the hallway with their research papers, Carol Levy, who feared a recurrence of the Holocaust in the rising conservative trend then coming up in America (Reagan would be elected in two years) set a backdrop by scrawling in Magic Marker in the stairwell a misquoted line from the Rolling Stones, "Now is the Time for Violent Revolution."

The girls were rowdy. They knocked out ceiling panels just to see the dust fly. They broke windows to hear the glass shatter. To offend any hapless and genteel innocent who came by, they posted a sign on their bathroom door: "Where Women Pee and Bathe." Mark Cline, who would form the band Love Tractor, lived on the fourth floor of Reed, and when he came down to the subbasement he and the girls pasted pornography on the walls and sat smoking cigarettes, carving genitalia into Barbie dolls. The girls were impressed with Mark because he knew how to play "Rock Lobster" on the guitar and they thought that was just so cool. They played The B-52's single twenty times in a night. None of them had ever seen The B-52's before, so when the band played at Memorial Hall that November 1978 everybody went.

Also that year, as The B-52's set a trend for lunacy in Athens, a student inspired by The Unknown Comic, a semi-cult figure of the late seventies from Chuck Barris' original *Gong Show*, put a bag over his head and ran for president of the student government at UGA. It was a sign of the times: a symptom of the craziness. He called himself The Unknown Candidate. He won and was listed in *Esquire* magazine's Dubious Achievement Awards in January 1979.

During the student government elections of 1979, the year after The Unknown Candidate was elected, a student ran for president on the Abolitionist ticket. He claimed student government was a charade, a resume-packing romp for overachievers. He promised to abolish student government if elected. He was elected. And he kept his promise. And the University of Georgia was without student government for nearly ten years after that. Following the election of 1979 and the abolition of student government, the successful candidate shifted the energies of his political machine to an even more important campaign, one that everybody could support: to get beer sold on campus.

■ ■ ■

In January 1979, at the beginning of winter quarter, Linda Hopper came back to Athens and took her room assignment in the sub-basement. Once there, she saw that something had happened in the year she had been away; everything had changed. She came back still wearing concert T-shirts and blue jeans, her long hair still straight and mousy brown, and her musical taste still faithful to the high school canon of Todd Rundgren and Led Zeppelin. What she saw when she returned was Sandi and Carol and Kathy and Kathleen O'Brien dancing around the dorm rooms in black-and-white saddle oxfords or their old cheerleader boots, their shiny hair now colored and tied in high ponytails. The rooms of the "subwaste-ment" and a few other rooms across campus sounded, muffled through the hallways, the new stuff of Elvis Costello and Patti Smith, segued in with hilarious nostalgic Monkees, the Archies, the Beatles, and James Brown. And the girls were dancing! Most middle-class white kids don't dance while growing up—maybe mimic some formal prom clutching—but not this kind of ecstatic thrash where the guys humped girls' legs and the girls lifted up their dresses on Mark Cline's command.

Mark Cline's friend Glenn Chitlik, who would become Love Tractor's manager, became the first "off-campus connection" for the girls in the subbasement who called themselves the D Phi U's and even had their own jerseys, pairing little sister to big brother with Chitlik and Cline and some others who called them-selves the Psi Chi O's. The Defy You girls found a safe haven away from the university in the Psychos' apartment off campus.

"We had a lot of acid parties," Chitlik remembers. "And we made movies. People came over and we had 'World Premier' parties where we showed these bad Super-8 movies that we made. At the World Premier parties we would drink a lot of beer and then hit this click and everyone would take their clothes off. But it wasn't an orgy. It never became an orgy. Maybe people snuck off, but it was just straightforward clean fun. Here we're all young and we're all beautiful, and everybody looked great and we would get naked.

"The first time it happened, everybody was drunk or tripping and we just decided to get naked. We went into the bedroom and got in a circle and one by one we jumped in the middle
and got felt up. The art teacher Jim Herbert was there and shouting, 'This is great! This is just like the sixties!' "

Everyone was cooperative and congenial during the naked parties and only a few times did weirdo guys stay around with their
clothes on just trying to see naked girls. When the unwanted hung
around the crowd staged elaborate routines to get rid of them, the
host yawning publicly, "Yawn! Boy, it's time for everybody to go.
Thanks a lot for coming!" And they all left, and with them the
undesirables. But then the cool people drove around the block and
came back and they all stripped and carried on with the party.

It was through Mark Cline and Glenn Chitlik that the rest-
less girls in the subbasement made their first foray off the campus and into the party music scene then starting up good in
town. That spring they heard through the party rumor circuit
that there was a band gonna play at a loft downtown late at
night: a band called Pylon: and it was gonna be pretty cool.

When the businesses in downtown Athens closed at night,
the only people on the streets were drifters and hookers in bond-
age gear. The empty streets of a closed-up town were of little
interest to most students at Georgia, who preferred well-lighted
places like T.K. Harty's, or the B & L Warehouse. A homemade
rock show up the narrow stairs of a downtown building filled
with fanciful artists in eccentric dress was not the average Georgia student's idea of a good time. But the crowd of kids in Reed
Hall that season—Bill Berry, Mark Cline, Carol Levy, the girls in
the subbasement, and a clutch of others—weren't your average
Georgia students. They were scenemakers.

13

PYLON GOES OUT OF TOWN — PYLON SEALS THE DEAL WITH NEW YORK CITY

Spring, 1979: The B-52's are waiting to accept a record deal. The subbasement of Reed Hall smells of burning rope, and up on the fourth floor Bill Berry, Mike Mills, and some of their wild-ass friends from Macon are spending weekends with a massive Peavy amp propped in the window of Bill's dorm room, blaring The Ramones down onto the heads of unsuspecting and dazed frat boys playing softball. Pylon, the new talk of the young scene, has played three parties. They are scheduled to play their fourth:

Before the party, Pylon's singer Vanessa asks her friend Craig Woodall to ask The B-52's' Fred Schneider to come see her band at a party. Fred had roomed with Craig in an apartment near the laundry room at some apartments in Athens' Five Points neighborhood. Craig asks Fred. Fred says sure, he loves parties.

He goes.

The party was ten miles east of town in Oglethorpe County, at the old brick house rented by a friend of Michael Lachowski's from the art school. It was Pylon's fourth time playing: their fourth party. A house, a keg, a band, a party; the practice was fast becoming tradition. Pylon played, and that night the crowd decided they liked them. The kids voted with their thrash, and they danced so hard the floor bowed and bucked and sucked the wind in and out of the room. The wind lifted the hair and skirts of girls near the windows, cooled the sweat on the shorthaired boys standing by the walls, and splashed the beer from your cup even when you stood still. Nowhere was there ground that didn't shake.

After the party Pylon gave Fred a copy of a demo tape and he took it to New York City. There he played it for Jim Fouratt, who booked the club Hurrah. Fouratt had been intrigued with The B-52's and had asked them if there were any other native bands in Athens. Fouratt heard Pylon's tape, thought them neat and charmingly naive.

"They're from Athens, too?" he exclaimed when he heard the tape. "What is it down there?"

On the strength of the tape and the word of The B-52's, Fouratt booked Pylon in August as the opening act for The Gang of Four, that season's hot new British sensation opening an American tour.

Vic Varney, twenty-six, worked with Michael Lachowski and Vanessa at DuPont, the textile mill on the edge of town that gave high-paying work to a handful of Athens artists. During idle times at work, Lachowski complained to Vic how doing a band wasn't all just fun and glory; he hated the business end of it. He just wanted to play. Vic, who had been playing keyboards with The Tone Tones, handled the public relations for that band and he knew a little about "booking gigs." He told Lachowski that he would manage Pylon, book them gigs, and all they had to do was cover the phone bill. Lachowski said hell, yeah.

After Fouratt booked Pylon for the New York show at Hurrah, Vic got on the phone. He was good on the phone. He called

The Hot Club in Philadelphia, where The Gang of Four was also scheduled to play. He went to work chatting up the club owner in his Chattanooga fiddler's twang.

"Hey, they're opening in New York for the Gang, why don't you have them open in Philly too?" he said, and he got them on the bill at The Hot Club. To round out what he'd quickly, in the course of half a pack of Camels and a phoner to Philly, started to call Pylon's first "Northeast Tour," Vic called The Ratt in Boston. The Gang of Four wasn't playing there, but Vic figured he would use the momentum he had.

"You haven't heard of Pylon? These guys are big news. They're opening for The Gang of Four in New York and Philly, why don't you . . ."

. . . and he got them a date at The Ratt—as the headliner. It would be their third date out of town and they were headlining at the biggest club in Boston. "This is so easy!" They had played only five parties in Athens by the time they played New York City.

For their first mini-tour of the Northeast that August, Vic and Michael drove up in Vic's Newport. Before the drive they bought and taped some singles to play on the way to New York City. That was the first time Lachowski heard The Gang of Four.

At Hurrah that night Vanessa saw for the first time green hair and everything, "just like I'd seen in the magazines." Someone bumped into her and knocked her down. Aghast, she chirped curious, "Why'd you do that?"

"We're dancing. It's called the West Coast Shove."

"The West Coast Shove?" said the on-stage dervish and off-stage belle. "I don't like it!"

Vic thought Pylon was much better than The Gang of Four. But of course he hadn't even watched The Gang of Four. He'd been too atwitter, talking up the band, telling tales of Athens. "Solidifying the achievement," he called it.

The response Pylon got in New York was overwhelming. Everybody was amazed, yet again, by a new Athens band. The show led to some good press:

"The Gang of Four was great as was Pylon, the first Georgia band to hit town since The B-52's, a tough act to follow, but Pylon is also a credit to their community," Glenn O'Brien wrote in *Interview*. "There's not much resemblance to The B's, although the guitarist has real classy taste in licks that is reminiscent of Ricky Wilson's. Pylon has a charming chanteuse up front, sort of a Georgia Georgie Girl, who manages to carry off several different postures including kooky, endearing, sincere, and wry. And not all the songs sound the same. . . . Recommended."

In his column O'Brien also declared that "those kids must listen to dub for breakfast." High praise, sure. Only thing was, nobody in Pylon knew what dub was. They went back to Athens to ask someone what it meant.

They got good press, but their stage presence was weak. The only person who moved was Curtis. Jim Fouratt took them aside after the show at Hurrah and told them, "Look, you've got to move around more on stage. I know what you're trying to do, that 'Just let the music stand on its own' thing. But it doesn't work. You need to *move*."

They all thought about how The Gang of Four rampaged on stage like wild animals just let out of cages. They talked about it and figured Fouratt was right. Vanessa hadn't yet memorized the songs, so she stood before a music stand on which she propped her lyric sheets. After they decided to change their stage presence and their attitude, Lachowski told Vanessa to go for it. From then on when she thrashed she knocked down the music stand and the papers flew all over the stage and onto the dance floor. But by that time she didn't need the lyric sheets. They just kept the stand because they liked the idea of a singer needing notes.

When they turned Vanessa loose, it happened. Overnight. It gelled. Suddenly the people who previously liked them, loved them. And those people who loved them were the people they wanted to reach, the sanctifiers of cool: In New York City they were immediately appreciated.

Pylon confirmed the reputation of Athens that had been swelling, slowly spreading, since The B-52's appeared the year before. Pylon sealed the deal between Athens and New York City.

From then on, for the rest of the new bands that would come up from Athens, Manhattan was their candy store.

THE CHURCH — PETER BUCK AND MICHAEL STIPE — THE PUNK GIRLS OF LEXINGTON HIGHWAY

About a third of the way up steep-sloped Oconee Street from the Oconee River, toward the hilltop spread of downtown Athens, was an old church. The outside was a chipping, half-painted stucco, all the sacred fixtures long since removed. On each side of the church the brief bit of yard was grown up with uncut, untended grass, vines, and young trees. In that thick brush was brick rubble and broken rock, whiskey bottles, plastic and paper carton stuff that the rain over a year had soaked and, soaking, wrapped around pieces of rock, splashed with dirt, and left to be covered by a season's leaf litter.

Rising up out of that lot was the church.

Inside, the once-sacred space had been desanctified by a realtor's makeover: Where the promise of the infinite and the everlasting once resided, there now was but an interior remodeled so thoroughly with Nu-built walls (wood-grain panels) that the one-time Episcopalian temple was indistinguishable on the inside from any ranch-style suburban home. The stairs going up to the second floor were wall-to-walled with carpet. A whole new house had been inserted in the shell of the church. The only way to be part of the original church from the inside was to go through a boarded-up window or a passageway punched through the wall in a closet of a bedroom. That punched hole was the transit from the profane 4 BR w/bath & w-w cpt into the old sanctuary, where, in the cavernous, broken-floored space, there had once stood an altar and where, now, stood nothing.

That summer of 1979 Dan Wall, who owned Wuxtry, the used record store, moved out of the church. He told an employee of his, Peter Buck, that if he wanted it he could have the lease. Peter said sure, why not, and he took the lease and moved into the church that fall with his brother, Ken, the girl he was see-ing—Kathleen O'Brien, that sanpaku subbasement refugee—and Peter's new friend he had met downtown that summer: this guy: this weird, quiet, curly-headed kid with acne who hung around the record store looking for 12" singles: Michael Stipe.

Peter Buck had come to Athens the year before, in 1978. Before coming to Athens Peter had lived in Atlanta and had gone to Emory University part-time. He worked at Doodah's, a record store near the Emory campus. The Bucks had lived in Atlanta since the early seventies, when they'd moved there from Cali-fornia. By 1978 Peter was tired of Atlanta. He hated the town. Hated his bosses. The feeling was mutual.

Peter hated a lot of things. He was sullen and quick-tempered. He spent most of his time reading, hanging out in record stores, and going to see bands. He had seen The Fans, The Nasty Bucks, all the seminal Atlanta activity. Peter played a little guitar. He had sat around in some rec rooms jamming, but everyone he met, their version of rock and roll was to do a Grateful Dead version of a Chuck Berry song with a limp back beat. They would do a noodly thing, clench their teeth, and look at the ceiling. Peter hated that shit.

One day he was at Atlanta's Wuxtry, another used record store, flipping through albums and talking to Mark Methe, who ran the store with his Athens-based partner Dan Wall. Peter complained that he didn't have a job and hated living with his parents. "I'm thinking about moving to Athens, 'cause my brother lives there," Peter mentioned. Mark Methe knew that Peter knew about records, so he pricked up his ears and said, "Well, a guy is quitting at the store in Athens in two days. You want a job?" And Peter said, "Great! Hell, yeah. Why not?" He did one day of training—instructions on how not to buy used Deep Purple albums—and moved to Athens.

Peter moved to town and lived with his brother Ken in a house out on Lexington Highway next to Marion and Buck's Bait Shop where worms, lizards, and double-ought fish hooks were sold. At the record store Peter worked forty hours a week for three dollars an hour—not a whole lot, but his rent was only fifty dollars a month. With a job at the Wuxtry, Buck found himself by stroke of good fortune working in the middle of the nascent scene. Wuxtry was at least "semi-hip," as Peter would say through the next many years. Before long he was friends with every guy in town who had ambitions to be guitar-cock in a band, and he was first-name and tattoo familiar with every girl who had a related ambition. There was constant talk of what was what and what everyone thought. Of what they were doing. Of how they were starting bands. These folks hung out at the record store looking for interesting new releases, digging up cool obscure stuff, finding new friends, listening to Peter tell them obscure rock trivia and stories about who and what he hated and who and what he loved, who and what he thought the greatest and where to get the best drugs.

It was through the record store, it would be said and said again through the coming many years, that Peter Buck met Michael Stipe. . . .

They met and they made quite the couple, doing their Mick

Jagger/Keith Richards thing: Peter had the perfect leer, Michael had the perfect pout.

Michael Stipe came to Athens in 1977, moving to the area from St. Louis, Mo., with his two sisters, Cindy and Linda, and his mom and retired military dad. Being the only boy, Michael was adored by his sisters and his parents. As a child he became accustomed to getting attention, and by the time he was a teen he knew that he was special, the main attraction.

At high school in St. Louis, Michael wore his hair in a natural, walked in platform shoes, wore wide-collared shirts. Despite all that, he was very popular. He was in a band and worked the glitter Mott the Hoople style: Once he went to *The Rocky Horror Picture Show* in Frank N. Furter drag: bare-chested and complete with black stockings, garters, bikini underwear, and thick lipstick, a Blue Oyster Cult pin stuck to his overcoat.

Michael tried very hard. He was working his way through it. He wanted to perform, and yet . . . he also wanted to be an artist. He could be flamboyant and flashy, or withdrawn, sultry, poetic. He was, by his own frequent confession, a confused Midwestern boy. But one thing he was sure of: He wanted to be a star.

Once in Athens, Michael looked for anything that would allow him to get up on stage. He wanted to be in another band. Wanted it bad. He worked in the kitchen at Sambo's, and between burger plates he hunched like an oil-lamp clerk over the back-page ads of the local paper, looking for the magic, future-fame-promising words: "Singer Wanted." That was what he did: Michael sang.

He answered ads. Went once. Saw they played shit. Never went back.

Finally he found one he could work with. A guitar player named Derek Nunally had a band called Gangster, which practiced in the garage behind his parents house in Monroe, Ga., a few miles outside of Athens. Michael practiced with the band in the garage, which they nicknamed "The Gangster Hideaway."

When they performed, playing all covers from Tom Petty to Elvis, they wore zoot suits. Michael, who was just seventeen at the time, wore one and gave himself a stage name, Michael Valentine. When they played around Athens his sisters were always there, his biggest fans.

"I did it for the money," Stipe said a decade later, still ashamed. "They paid me well. But it's deeply embarrassing. It was a step back, just a reaching out for anything. I wore some elephant bells I had from high school and they all thought I was serious."

Gangster broke up after Michael had been with them for a year. That was all right by him. He was into new music:

"My folks had gotten a Publisher's Clearinghouse thing, you know, pick ten magazines for a dollar? And they said 'Pick anything you want,' and so I got *The Village Voice*. It sounded better than *Good Housekeeping, Boys' Life* or *Sports Illustrated*. It sounded different. So I got it and started reading about all this stuff going on at CBGB's. And I read an article by a writer comparing the new music to black-and-white television. Grainy, as opposed to the real high-resolution color television. And it was, like, all these new bands were small black-and-white TV against color. And it really piqued my interest. At the time I bought records at the mall and the PX, and the PX carried Roxy Music. I would go into the mall and bug the guy for records and finally Patti Smith's record came out and I bought it.

"I loved Patti Smith. When I was sixteen my girlfriend gave me a membership in the Patti Smith Fan Club and her mother ran it and she sent me long letters and snapshots and wished me a happy sixteenth birthday."

When he first came to Athens and enrolled in the university as an art student, Michael lived outside of town. When he had time between and after classes he hung out at Wuxtry talking to Peter, or at Chapter Three, another record store downtown. Between that, working at Sambo's, and playing in Gangster, his time was spent.

Once they moved into the church together, the social worlds of Peter and Michael expanded. It was the fall of 1979 and a new school year was beginning. And it began with an invitation to a party. . . .

Four of the D Phi U girls—Sandi Phipps, Linda Hopper, Kathy Russo, and Sally Hamilton—had moved out of the subbasement of Reed Hall when school let out that spring '79. When school started again in the fall they set up house off-campus in a four-bedroom rental east of town on Lexington Highway, out across from the Putt Putt miniature golf course, just down the highway a ways from the church where their friend Kathleen had just moved with Peter Buck and Michael Stipe. The girls were thrilled to be free from the dorm. They spent the first days of the new fall finding old friends from the year before, collecting the new season's phone numbers. To help out the re-meeting, they threw a party.

They called it a Reggae Party.

They prepared all afternoon:

Sandi and Kathy set up a grill on the back porch. Sally picked up the keg and borrowed Peter Tosh records. Linda rolled spleefs. They braced the speakers in the living room and moved the stereo into a back bedroom where the turntable could best be kept steady during the floor-bending dancing that they knew was soon coming. They tore chicken wire from a fence out back, looped it into lopsided go-go cages and tied them with bits of ribbon like the bits they tied into their tight-braided whitegirl dreadlocks. They painted their eyes and mouths with a punk bruise smear of purple and black. They slipped red T-shirts over the lamps in the rooms and dimmed the lights to a disco-whorehouse low. . . .

It was their first week back at school and none of them had slept in days.

They announced the party and word went around town: the D Phi U house . . . across from the Putt Putt . . . free beer.

In that past August Pylon had played New York City with
The Gang of Four. In early September they played the Agora
Ballroom in Atlanta with Talking Heads and The B-52's. Pylon
was getting great reviews. They were special. They were the heroes in town, becoming a scene. Mark Cline, who was friends
with the girls from Reed Hall, had made friends with *That Crowd*
the year before: The Tone Tones, Pylon, the art school kids:
Them. That first weekend back at school, Mark told them all that
he knew these girls who were having a party. "And they know
how to party! Trust me." And they headed out the highway to
the house. The intown art school band crowd showed up at the
D Phi U house and mixed with the party-girl freshkids and their
assorted friends, the blue-jeaned hippies, and the satellite cluster
of shirt-tucked boys who always hover round a house of babes.
It was the first seriously great episode of crowd-mixing.

The D Phi U girls couldn't believe the weirdo friends Mark
Cline brought with him to the party, new rock hipsters in peg-
legged black cords and polka-poly party dresses. The girls freaked,
but they loved it. David Gamble, big-chested, broad-shouldered,
shaved-headed, shirtless drummer with The Tone Tones, Athens' second band, was the only one who really scared anybody.
Gamble got hugely drunk that night and Mark Cline, the devil
himself in dead-man silver white lipstick, scratched a swastika on
the big one's forehead with black mascara. Gamble sat through
the party in the D Phi U girls' big pink thrift-store chair drinking
beer from a gallon jug. With his shiny shaved head, no shirt, and
the mascara swastika drip-spinning from sweat, Gamble looked
like the closest thing to a real punk any of the new kids had ever
seen.

Although it was called a Reggae Party and the girls did their
hair in thematic dreds, they only played one side of a Peter Tosh
album. After that they kept on with the New Wave dance stuff:
Talking Heads, Elvis Costello, Blondie. That pissed off the mud-
booted dope growers, who hadn't yet come to appreciate the
return of three-chord rock.

The night came on and the swill of partyers filled the yard, the kitchen, the bedrooms. In the living room a multi-colored hammock was bolted from the front door frame to the wall. It supported five easily if they wrapped themselves tight and didn't move around too much. That night the hammock stayed full, swung hard, stayed hung.

Bill Berry and Mike Mills showed up and they each kept falling in love repeatedly throughout the night with the host-esses, while newly met lovers took turns in the bathrooms, cheered on by Mark Cline's coterie of nasty Catholic rudeboys who pounded on the bathroom door and took names and right then started some slanders that would go around Athens for years to come, tales of who did what to whom in the bathroom that early fall night.

The dancing crowd, hot, sweaty, drunk, filled the living room, dining room, bedrooms. Everyone took their turns dancing in the chicken-wire go-go cages, then took a break for a beer, stood in the crowded kitchen, leaned on the counters, stained shirts and dresses with the countertop spills.

Someone had bought a flourescent plastic tube at the county fair and it got out in the crowd somehow. As a group the kids dancing in the living room passed it mouth-to-mouth: Girls and guys in turns took the five-inch stick in their teeth, passed it on, and paused with strangers over the exchange. When trad-ing it, they lingered over a dance-floor kiss, eyes closed, hips thrusting, each deep-throating the lighted green-yellow carnival favor, one taking it from another after a slow wet slip, then look-ing for their choice to pass it next, deciding who to give the glow, with whom to meet lips, share spit, click teeth.

The next day, the girls who lived at the house woke to a scene of such stained devastation that they hauled carpet and furniture into the front yard and set them afire.

LIFE AT THE CHURCH — THE METHOD ACTORS

The church became party central: Day and night, sleazy drug dealers came and went, fueling the weekend marathons and spoiling everybody for the next week's classes; friends and acquaintances stopped by to test their endurance against these maximal partyers. Kathleen, whose circle of friends was quite diverse, welcomed everyone.

Peter, the sullen one, when he slept at the church and not at the house of some newly met babe, most days slept late on his upstairs bedroom foam-pad pallet, surrounded by fly-nesting Budweiser cans, dog-eared paperback rock histories, and Raymond Chandler novels. He'd wake up late, knock a book of Nietzsche from his pillow, and walk downtown for a breakfast of goat barbeque at Strickland's restaurant. The kitchen sink at the church was full of dirty dishes, the garbage can overflowed with fast-food packaging, and the refrigerator stank of unappetizing remainders of infrequent attempts at domestic feeding. The church was a place to party or crash, not really to live.

Michael Stipe was fast becoming an unwitting ringleader of art school kids with the new americanpunk attitude. He was working with fluorescent paint and styrofoam, crayon shavings, wax paper, and xeroxed photographs. Michael brought his new friends to the church after, say, a Friday afternoon color theory class and they played new records, popped open beers, and broke the tax tape on bottles of whiskey. Sandi Phipps, Linda Hopper, Mark Cline, all sorts of folk hung, sweated, danced, and drank at the church. When it got late and dark and they'd drunk enough, they cut ruination into each others' hair and then headed into town, teeth clenched and vision-smeared, prepped to freak.

Up the Oconee Street sidewalk they stumbled and tripped, sometimes defying gravity, often becoming its victim. Peter, Michael, and the girls slow-crawled up the hill, brushing cut hair from their shoulders and singing, "When you're a Jet you're a Jet all the way," waking neighbors, and setting dogs to barking, but none worrying because, "Hey, don't worry, Peter's got a knife. Hey Pete, show us yer knife!" On quaalude legs they all make it to the theater for a movie. They can't stay in their seats. They slide and fidget and fall to their knees. Then out again. First to the Majik Market for another six-pack and half pint, then back to the church. It's not a home, just a shelter, a degraded limbo.

One day early in the fall quarter Paul Lombard visited the church. Paul had lived in the basement of Reed Hall the year before, knew the girls from the subbasement, and that fall had moved with some friends into another house farther out Lexington Highway. Paul, who would play a wizard guitar and sing in a number of Athens bands to come, could be trouble sometimes, and he was trouble when he went that day to the church. One thing led to another and Paul called Peter a faggot. Peter got mad, punched a wall that should have been Paul, hurt his hand, but scared Paul into leaving, beer bottles whizzing past his head. After Paul left someone at the church spray-painted "Paul is Dead" on the church's front-door canopy. And Peter declared, "Fag? Fag? How can he call me a fag? I sleep with ten times as many women as he does!"

Peter was known to be bad, to carry a knife. Paul, when not trouble, was timid and scared. So Paul's roommate Harlan Hale, the same guy who loaned Kathleen O'Brien the snakeskin she wore for her performance with the WUOGerz when she first met Bill Berry, loaned Paul a knife. It was a commando-style dagger, ground to a good edge on both sides. Paul, ready for Peter, stuck the blade into the plywood floor by the side of his bed.

Peter never came. He forgot about the feud. And Paul forgot about the knife. One night Paul got up to pee, and walking to the bathroom he hit that blade full stride, catching the razor edge right between his big toe and the next. His roommates called up to the punk girls' house up the street and it took a bribe of a joint to get someone to give Paul a ride to the university infirmary. That trip from Lexington Highway to the infirmary would be made not just a few times during the coming year. But that was okay; they all loved the sight of blood.

On Halloween that year there was a party at the church. No band, just a costume party—one that was scheduled to catch the crowd after the local show. Earlier in the night a new band had debuted at Tyrone's, the only club in town booking the local original bands. The new band was made up of the remains of The Tone Tones, who had broken up earlier that summer. Vic Varney and David Gamble came together again after The Tone Tones dissolved, practiced once some songs Vic had written, and decided to try it again. They thought about adding more instruments, but with the memory of their experience with The Tone Tones still fresh in mind they nixed the idea; the more people involved with a band the more chance for interpersonal conflict,

they had learned. They kept the lineup at two and agreed on a
name: The Method Actors.

Vic was still booking Pylon's shows, so when it came time
for The Method Actors to debut they opened for Pylon at the
Halloween show at Tyrone's, playing a fast set of Vic's mad
scream and open-tuned guitar noise, backed with Gamble's mus-
cleman slam-drumming. At that show when Pylon went on Lachowski hooked his bass to a TV set and managed to coordinate
a vertical and horizontal black-and-white image while he played.
The stage lightshows—neon angles that buzzed the retina like
the drone bass buzzed bone, yet still flicked sharp like Bewley's
guitar—were done by Watt King, a highly respected local art
school prodigy. Pylon played sixteen songs that night and en-
cored with the theme from *Batman*.

After the show the handful of hip folk who had been to
Tyrone's left their cars parked where they were and walked down
the hill from Foundry Street to the church. Others from across
campus and town drove down and lined the side streets with
their cars. Inside the church the jam of bodies was thick, and
constant was their flow through the building: in the door, through
the bedroom, on your knees, through the hole in the closet and
into the back, into the sanctuary, where the keg was.

Jim Herbert, the art teacher, was there. He loved this new
excitement that sparked the kids. He came half-naked, his sharply
carved torso painted gold, like an Oscar in blue jeans and full
gray-black head of hair. Herbert stood around the church, proud
with a plastic cup of beer, and talked to the young art school
kids and asked the shapeliest and most daring-eyed of them if
they would like to be filmed. There were nymphs, pirates, Flannery O'Connor's "artificial niggers," and a Jimmy Carter pea-
nuthead with big teeth stuck in a presidential grin. Jerry Ayers
was there. Jerry, the early influence on Keith and Ricky of The
B-52's, came as a scarecrow: And his costume marked a departure in style.

Jerry was quieting, now quitting the campy drag that had

The B-52's
the Agora
Atlanta
ca 1981.

[Sandra-Lee Phipps]

Carol Levy,
Ingrid Schorr.

[Linda Hopper]

R.E.M. circa 1985
on the roof of
Ruthless Records
in downtown
Athens.

[Sandra-Lee Phipps]

Michael Stipe
at
169 Barber
Street.

[Linda Hopper]

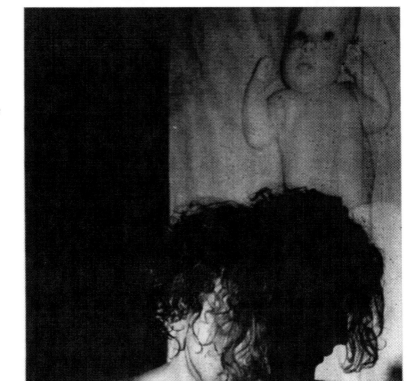

ichael Stipe
1981.

[nda Hopper]

**Early publicity
shot of R.E.M.**

[Sandra-Lee Phipps]

Michael Stipe at
169 Barber.

[Linda Hopper]

Two girls
at Tyrone's.

[Linda Hopper]

Bill Berry,
Ann Boyles, and
Ingrid Schorr
*(for whom M. Mills
wrote 'Rockville').*

[*Linda Hopper*]

Michael Stipe,
Mike Mills at
59 Barber
Street.

[*Linda Hopper*]

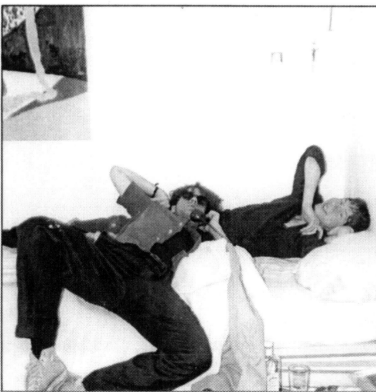

Go Van Go,
featuring,
from left,
Juan Molina,
Robert Warren,
Dana Downs
and
Vic Varney.

[Linda Hopper]

Oh-OK,
featuring,
from left,
David Pierce,
Linda Hopper,
and
Linda Stipe,
backstage at
Tyrone's.

[Linda Hopper]

slie Michel,
da Hopper
d
rk Phredd
kitchen
169 Barber
eet.

da Hopper

Jefferson Holt
(R.E.M. manager)
in the remains
of Tyrone's.

[Sandra-Lee Phipps]

Music School,
featuring,
from left,
Paul Lombard,
Joe Kuhl, and
Ken Buck,
in basement
of Stitchcraft.

Ann Boyles
and
Peter Buck,
Easter party,
1980.
169 Barber
Street

[Linda Hopper]

dressed The B-52's for their success. He was turning away from the audacious glitter fag assault and was now falling silent, retreating to mystery, a coyote trickster, but still pretty. That night Jerry was costumed in a way that the kids weren't used to costume: On him, the baggy rags with straw at his wrists looked normal. Sure enough he did have straw coming out of his torn shirt and slack pants; but it fit. Jerry's costume wasn't a sheet pulled over his head, wasn't a mask held to his face with a rubber band: He was the costume, it became him. It was a total becoming that made Jerry's bits great acting.

Michael Stipe saw Jerry Ayers that night. He watched him. He was intrigued.

Nobody knew it then but it was one of the final seasons of real freedom, before the onset of AIDS. You have twenty thousand human bodies at the peak of their health and youth. You have the distribution among the two biological sexes and innumerable ones of other dimensions. It was a heavily sexual time. Rutting in the dirt. At parties. In the bathrooms. Making somebody before passing out and then loving whomever you wake up next to, found by groping from floor to couch. The worst thing to worry about was herpes, but that scare didn't really hit too hard until the next year. But even with that negligible fear you can still just do it anyway. You meet somebody and you can just see it in their eyes and in fifteen minutes you are out in the car. But of course those were the radical times. In Athens then, all sense and safety was violated.

As the Halloween party went on late, went on crazy with all the kids having had their senses multiplied by some baggy-stashed and back-bedroom-bought alchemy, where dizziness was free thanks to cigarette smoke and beer, where the wank of love and lust gave the fine polished edge of true lunacy to the mass hysteria . . . there, then, Peter Buck and Michael Stipe wrestled together in the kitchen, knocked over the table of empty snack bowls, and sparked the crowd into an explosion that trashed the place.

By night's end, day's beginning, a tangle of folk ended up crowding the bathroom, eyes all MDA-aglitter and handing back and forth in delirium a giant makeup sampler kit of one hundred shades: Bellowing, shrieking, they hauled in people against their will, painted them with Maybelline and cut their hair for good measure. It was heavily physical, with laughing-strength fights and thuds as girls held on hard to door frames while friends pulled them loose, then all falling onto the tile floors with screams as crotches are grabbed and dresses fly up, everyone and all demon-laughing in love with strangers they've just found themselves lying atop. They lined each others' eyes with the sampler kit makeup. They rouged each others' cheeks. On one poor girl they painted fingernail polish onto her nipples.

That was when Michael Stipe met Carol Levy: He crawled from the bathroom with a handful of lip gloss and smeared it into her face.

16

DB RECS — PYLON DOES A SINGLE

When Michael Lachowski and Randy Bewley first got the idea to start Pylon, they'd been listening to the new-music stuff— Dead Kennedys, The Clash, The Pretenders, Kraftwerk, The Sex Pistols—for a full year before 1978, and they thought for sure it was too late for another nowhere outfit to get together and, on the strength alone of gall and art, accomplish anything, make a name. They worried that the new music impulse was over. It was still happening, sure—Talking Heads, Elvis Costello—but it was too good. How could it last much longer? Such a vital surge, like the *unh* of a good party, can't go on forever. Despite the doubts they did it anyway, and on Valentine's Day 1979 Vanessa went carrying love-sacramental candy to practice with the boys in a dirty downtown studio and Pylon officially began.

And that year they saw the initial punk movement trans-formed and renewed as a fresh generic, New Wave—meaning nothing more than anything you wanted it to mean, so long as it wasn't hippie, fusion, or heavy metal. Bands were still releasing their debut hits on little 7″ 45-rpm singles but, again, doubt: Pylon never considered cutting a single themselves. To them, if someone was on a single they were from someplace else that was, like, real. Someplace established. Not Athens. They never thought that just anyone could do it, like, just get wax.

Then The B-52's did it. "And they're from here!" all said, surprised. As The B-52's "Rock Lobster/52 Girls" single went into more pressings (eventually selling seventeen thousand!) the street talk of that local combo's quick fab success in New York peddled itself through the art school's after-class gossip and chat. Then Pylon, too, as they played out, felt the sweet addictive lash of critical acclaim, the tickle of kind tongue—"Kooky, endearing, sincere, wry . . ."—just as the B's did after their first New York City trips— acceptance, quick, easy, head-spinning acceptance. Pylon saw the ready audience whose favor they had already won. Pylon thought about it. Pylon decided to do a single themselves.

"We asked the B's about it and they told us to talk to Danny Beard," Michael Lachowski said. "We asked him and he told us about how to do it, about studios, pressing and all that. We kept talking to him, asking how much it would cost and stuff like that and one day he said, 'You want me to put it out for you?' And we said, 'Hell, yeah.' "

Pylon was one of the new bands grounded in the belief that it was possible to change the face of rock and roll simply by mangling convention. It was a joyful vandalism, incompetence for its own sake.

"Our first single was just something Danny funded on his own," Lachowski says. "He let us do the artwork and everything and he took care of distributing it. We didn't have to pay him anything. We never made any money back, but we didn't care.

"Not until way later did we care."

Poly-panted Danny never thought about becoming a record magnate. He hardly kept accounts at his record store, and even with the healthy demand expressed for The B-52's single DB Recs was still little more than a label of convenience, a one-man source of subsidy for Danny's personal favorites. After "Rock Lobster/ 52 Girls," Danny never planned on putting out any more records. But sales were good and there was other talent around. Friends of his.

Although he contributed little to the production of the B's single, just sort of hung out in the studio, Danny credited Kevin Dunn as associate producer. Kevin was a friend. And talented too. He felt frustrated in The Fans, reconstituted since last year's mindblower with Mike Green. He felt his songs were being neglected. On The Fans' second single, Kevin got one cut. On the third single both songs were Alfredo's. So Danny did a single with Kevin: "Nadine" b/w "Oktyabrina."

In the Fall of 1979 the single was reviewed in the press, gathering a handful of three-inch, seven-point type favorable reviews in *New York Rocker, Trouser Press,* and *Interview:*

> "Kevin Dunn of Atlanta and The Fans has a really great, with-it single that's worth looking around for: 'Nadine'/'Oktyabrina' (DB Records). . . . Pick hit of, uh, last week."
>
> December, 1979
> *Interview*

With the B's single and then with Dunn's, Danny's DB Recs became one of the most significant independent labels in America as the eighties came on.

The first night Pylon went in the studio they recorded "Feast on My Heart" and "Human Body." But they had just written a new song called "Cool" which they played while they were warming up, and they liked it, so they decided to use that one for the single instead of "Feast on My Heart." They had also written "Dub," a nod to Glenn O'Brien's reference in his early

Pylon review that they listened to dub for breakfast. They liked their two new songs, so they changed their plans and Pylon's first single became "Cool/Dub."

It wasn't until Pylon went into the studio that Curtis Crowe was convinced that Vanessa was right for the band. Until that point he could never hear what she was doing because they always played through bad PAs with bad monitors. He knew she was doing something. When he finally heard it, all his doubts about the band were vanquished.

The single in the can, they scheduled it for release in January 1980:

PYLON 45—"Cool/Dub"

"Representing rural raucousness, recording righteous racket, rocking really rampant, ready righton rogues release rip-roaring robust rollicking rolypoly record right now.

"Never knowing the meaning of the word nix, another effort graces your desk having utilized the same studio, engineer, producer, and distributor that brought forth The B-52's 'Rock Lobster' and Kevin Dunn's 'Nadine.' PYLON from hep capital Athens, Georgia has laid down two songs written by the band in their first vinyl effort. Members Vanessa Ellison, Michael Lachowski, Randall Bewley, and Curtis Crowe vary in age from 23 to 24, and played their first public show in Athens at the 40 Watt Club in March 1979."

DB Recs Press Release
January 1980

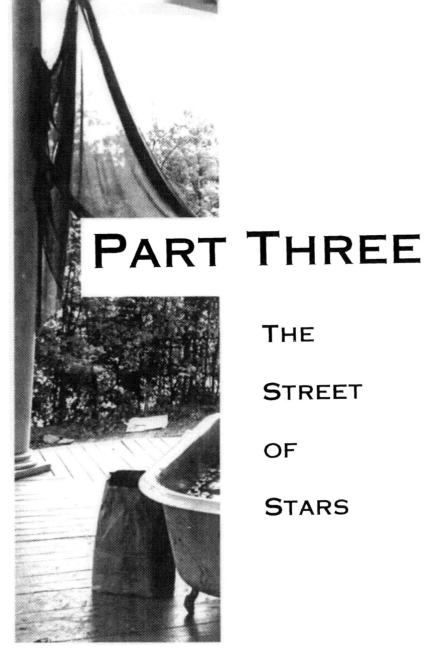

PART THREE

THE

STREET

OF

STARS

17

PETER BUCK AND MICHAEL STIPE MEET BILL BERRY AND MIKE MILLS — R.E.M. DEBUTS — BILL DROPS OUT OF SCHOOL

Through the winter of 1979–1980, as The B-52's and Pylon made "Athens" a New York City buzzword, Peter Buck and Michael Stipe sat around in the church, slowly working up their own act. Peter fingered chords on his black-and-white Rickenbacker—A-C-D—while Michael gripped his broken pencil piece and tacked together phrases for lyrics, classic pop concepts that he dredged from the depths of his late-night radio memories, working feverishly to purge himself of all the clichés he'd heard growing up, to free himself to express his own visions: "Living in cities, living in cars, living the way you never wanted to . . . Shaking it up, shaking it down, shaking the ways you always wanted to . . ."

Peter and Michael were already hip to their Mick and Keith routine; everybody noticed it: Michael with the ragged, sensual, scarf-wrapped poet look; Peter with his sharp-faced scowl, tight black jeans, and dangling skull-and-crossbones earring. Together the two of them killed many early dark afternoons sitting by heaters, talking rock, and watching *Bewitched*, since Peter had a lusty crush on Sabrina, Samantha's bad-girl cousin in sixties psychedelic minis. When not watching that or *The Beverly Hillbillies*, they jammed on a verse-chorus riff thirty-five times in a row: "G-L-O-R-I-A ..." and tossed their empty Budweiser cans into wet-bottomed paper bags.

Peter enjoyed just doing that: drinking beer, listening to records, talking about cool shit, scanning PBS for Beatles documentaries. Although he had always thought about being in a band, he didn't think they would ever really do anything with the songs they were writing. But Michael had different ideas. He'd heard about The B-52's, he'd seen Pylon, seen The Method Actors; he knew it could be done. He couldn't do it himself, he needed support, and with Peter they just might pull it off. His high school dream still possessed him, and he felt that in his collaboration with Peter he had lucked into something good, something great.

"I had to coerce Peter into doing stuff," Michael Stipe recalled later about his prep time in the church. "He had this feeling that everyone in rock bands were egotistical assholes. Plus, he couldn't play guitar to save his life. We did play with some other people once. Dan Wall, who lived in the church before we did, would come over and play bass and saxophone, and some other guy played drums. We set up in the church and played a couple times, but that was about it."

Their roommate Kathleen knew that Peter and Michael wanted to be in a band, so she also applied some pressure. She knew that Bill Berry had free time from the WUOGerz, so she told them that they should meet.

"We met Bill at a party," Stipe remembers. "I liked his eyebrows—*eyebrow*—and said that he was pretty cool. Then we went to Tyrone's one night and met Mills and I said, 'No *fucking way*.' He was wearing bellbottoms and a stupid haircut. But it was a bargain. If we take Bill we take Mike."

At first, after meeting at Tyrone's, the local club that was starting to book the local bands like Pylon and The Method Actors, the four guys kept saying they would get together but nothing ever happened.

"It's pretty funny," Bill recalls. "Twice we were supposed to get together and jam but we never did. It seemed like it was never going to happen. But then I saw Pete at Tyrone's one night and said let's go for it one more time. And we did.

"I'm glad we did."

Bill borrowed the drums from the WUOGerz. Mike borrowed a bass.

"We first practiced in late February," says Mike. "It was cold. We didn't have any heat. It was in the back of the church. I was trying to play with gloves on and steam was coming out of our mouths. Bill and I had some songs from Macon. We'd messed around and put some songs together and we showed those to Peter and Michael, and we saw what they did with them and we thought, 'That's pretty cool. This is okay.' "

"They were all real wary of each other," Kathleen O'Brien recalls about the four guys who were playing in the back of the church. "They were all just so distrustful. I mean, talk about four different personalities. You've got Peter, Mr. Atlanta, cool, rock-and-roll guy; Michael, this introverted, insecure, displaced-in-the-south artist-type; and these two from Macon—Bill the badboy and Mike the good nerd kid. They were real different but they clicked. And the thing is, they never wanted it to click. They never wanted to acknowledge the fact that they were anything. That's why I went out of my way to coerce them to play at my birthday party. I said, 'Listen, two of you are my roommates, I'm dating one of you. If you want to make me happy, play at my birthday party.' And they did."

That night, April 5, 1980, it was Kathleen's party: for her and by her; she did it all. She wanted it to be big. She cleaned the house. She bolted the front doors and posted the sign, "Enter in Rear." She told everybody about the party. She reserved the kegs. To make the party extra special she even got a fancy tap: lighted, fake woodgrain fleur-de-lis-shaped Budweiser tap— putting down a bad check as deposit. And she got the bands to play.

Not only were her roommates (Buck, Stipe) practicing in a band, but across town there was another crew setting up: The Side Effects:

Kathleen knew Paul Buchard from Atlanta, having met at a German Club camp one summer. Paul was playing drums with Kit Swarz, his roommate, when they met Jimmy Ellison, the husband of Vanessa, the lead singer for Pylon. Jimmy was twenty-eight—older than everyone else—but he was still a bop boy, still a kid like the rest. His wife of three years was out of town a lot, traveling with her band. With her on the road, flush full of fame and oats, their young marriage wore thin and failed. During the days of their separation Jimmy wandered through parties, weeping after a few beers, looking for a hug. To get his mind off the agony he started playing bass with Paul and Kit in The Side Effects.

Kathleen knew they had been practicing. She asked them to play. She had her roommates' band and The Side Effects; she rounded out a three-act night with another local band called Turtle Bay.

Through the circuit—record stores, road talk, radio station—word went out about the party. "Park down that side street, you know, turn off by the Jesus Saves sign just before the river. Or park in the big lot by the river, you know, by O'Malley's. Park up in town, if you have to, and walk down the hill to the church. You know, that church down Oconee where they have those killer parties." "Where that cute guy from Wuxtry lives?" "Yeah, him. That's the place."

The church filled.

Again, like the body twists and tail flicks that choreograph a school of fish, like with rumors and the language of crowds, inside the church word got around: "Through the hole in the closet. Go through the hole in the closet." That was where the fun was.

The crowd in the bedroom mills and wonders and stands patiently, waiting in line to crawl one by one through the hole in the closet and into the sanctuary. Once in the back word goes around to keep to the right, the boards on one side are rotten: Keep off, or risk a leg, ankle, worse. Everyone who made it into the back was drunk, stoned, or tripping, yet still wise enough to stay away from the broken floor.

On the makeshift stage the bands play and drone. The crowd shifts and rotates, clusters round, then circulates out again, back through the slow flowing hole and up into the bedrooms, looking for the brother with the MDA, looking for a joint to silence the ringing in its ears, waiting in line to pump more beer from the kegs.

"Ahhhhhh ahh ahh ahh ahhmm not your stepping stone, not your steppin' stone, not your steppin' stone. . . ." an unnamed band sings, and the crowd stands and watches, some wince, as Peter practices his first tentative twirls and Michael hangs onto the microphone like he would for the next swift decade, entrancing a stunned and surprised audience.

The crowd that night wasn't one of fans, they're strangers and friends, beer hogs and party hounds, students on a mission to make as much noise as they can before having to go back to class. The members of the bands that played weren't stars, weren't ambitious rockers: They were just the latest to find out how much fun it was to play pretend with your friends: And that night they became the new kids in the scene, the latest to show that playing pretend is its own reality, the next generation of Athens bands after the B's, Pylon and The Method Actors.

By the end of the night someone had stolen the fancy Budweiser tap and Kathleen lost her deposit.

After the tap was stolen at the party Kathleen had to make good her deposit. The guys in the band decided to help her out.

When Mike Hobbs from Tyrone's, the club in town where Pylon and The Method Actors were now begrudged modestly but intensely attended Wednesday nights, asked them to play a show, they agreed. They needed to make some money to pay for the taps. To warm up, they played for free at a fundraiser for Rick the Printer's 11:11 Koffee Klub.

At the end of Washington Street on the edge of downtown, Rick Hawkins had rigged an empty space with a coffee bar and some hotplates. He called it the 11:11. It's slogan was "Do you know where your coffee cup is?" Rick had come to Athens in the early seventies. By the time he was twenty he owned a building near the Oconee River where he set up his Volkswagen repair and print shop, and which became a listed welcoming hostel for any wastrel hippie Rainbow Family member who wandered through Athens.

The Koffee Klub was where the kids went to hang out, sample bohemian decay. Coffee was speed to the nineteen-year-olds who rendezvoused at the dark dingy space to prepare for their nightly ventures into the underground. Coffee became the object of a cult, and its sipping became a ritual. At the Koffee Klub the only record played on the toy stereo there was "Heartbreak Hotel." Over and over.

Before the band played at the Koffee Klub they finally gave themselves a name. They figured if there were going to be posters they needed to call themselves something. They rejected all that they considered: Twisted Kites, Cans of Piss, Slut Bank, The Male Nurses. Then Michael Stipe started flipping through the dictionary. He knew that had been the technique used to name the Dadaists and he figured that was good enough for them. He poked his finger onto a page. "How about R.E.M.?" he asked as they all sat around the church.

"What's it mean?" Mills asked.

"Says here 'Rapid Eye Movement,' " Stipe said, "but we can just use R.E.M." "Sure. Okay. Why not?" Peter said. That was it. They had a name.

During the show at the Koffee Klub a guy watched from the audience. It was Bertis Downs, a law student who didn't want to practice law. Bert had already met Bill on the Contemporary Concerts committee and he had met Peter at the Wuxtry because they both were Neil Young fans and Peter would turn him on to obscure bootlegs and new releases. Bert was loving it. He loved it up to the point that the police came in response to a noise complaint and shut the club down.

After the plug was pulled by the cops Bert pulled Peter aside. Bert went up to him and said, "Man, ya'll are going to be big. Bigger than the Beatles. I mean it, man. *I swear!*"

Peter sneered, chuckled and said, "Yeah, right."

There was Bert Downs, this crazy law student, saying R.E.M. was going to be bigger than big. The cops had just left, all around them people were drinking coffee with curdled milk and bourbon, and Bert kept repeating a prophesy that this band which had just been silenced by the law would someday be bigger than the Beatles.

All Peter could say was, "Who's got a beer?"

In May R.E.M. opened for the Brains, the Atlanta band led by Tom Grey, who had filled in for Mike Green on keyboards during The Fans L.A. fiasco two years earlier. Athens critics on the school paper claimed R.E.M. blew The Brains away. Atlanta critics, however, claimed that that opinion was just another expression of the pro-Athens chauvinism felt by the town since The B-52's, Pylon, and The Method Actors had appeared. The debate was never settled. It just widened the rift between the two cities.

In June, Peter's brother Ken moved out of the church. Bill and Mike started staying there.

"I stopped going to classes and school just slipped away," Bill recalls of those first few months of being in the band. "I think I kind of wanted it to happen. Like habitual criminals who want to go to jail so they don't have to do anything. I think that's what it was. I despised school, and what was going on was so exciting that it was hard to get up for first-period class.

"It's funny; I came to school to grow up and do something right, but I just said fuck it and I threw myself into the band.

"As soon as the university asked me to discontinue my affiliation with them, I got a job at the Holiday Inn as morning busboy. That really sucked. Here I was staying at the church and I had to get up at four A.M. to get the breakfast buffet set up. There would be parties still going on at the church and I would be dressed up in these brown polyester pants and Peter and Michael would be sitting there, wasted, drinking beer and laughing at me, saying:

"See ya, Bill. Heh heh heh."

Athens Gets Its First New Music Club, The 40 Watt East

"40 Watt Club Entertains Wavers on a Shoestring"
" 'The Baked Potato' and 'The Sardine' are not new
dances, but they do describe the heat and SRO crowds
at Athens' first, exclusively New Wave nightclub, The
40 Watt Club, located in what used to be the Crow's
Nest atop the downtown Sub and Steak Sandwich
Shop. . . .

The Red and Black
June 3, 1980

Paul Scales was a party boy from Macon, and he blew a little
harp, was working up a band of his own; everybody was doing
it: the B's, Pylon, and now R.E.M. Paul had been hanging around
Athens for a few years and by 1980 was working at the Sub and
Steak Sandwich Shop on the downtown corner of College and

Broad, across the street from the university's north campus, the greensward shaded by three-hundred-year-old oaks and waxy-leaved magnolias.

Upstairs above the sandwich shop was a space that until recently had been The Crow's Nest, a lounge-variety bar with a small stage. During its final days The Crow's Nest featured open-mike nights during which student bands played, desperate poets read. The B-52's' Kate Pierson had played folk songs up there. It had been closed for a year when Paul Scales saw it.

Scales was a friend of Curtis Crowe, Pylon's drummer. One day Curtis came back into town from playing New York City with Pylon and Scales said, "Man, Curtis, I've found this great spot for a rehearsal studio for my band."

They drank a few beers at the Sub and Steak and Scales took Curtis upstairs. They walked in. There was a bar, an old glass-front cooler, some tracked lights. Curtis thought to himself, "Okay, this is kind of nice." Then he remembered the success of his parties at his loft across the street. He said, "Paul, why don't we open up a nightclub? We can use the license from downstairs to sell beer and you can practice whenever the nightclub's closed. It'll give us a great place to hang out and drink beer."

Paul Scales said, sure, why not, and they talked to Bob Yudi who ran the sandwich shop. Yudi said they could sublet the space for seven hundred a month.

Paul and Curtis told him to forget that noise; seven hundred was outrageous. They negotiated, Curtis once again scamming. In the end they rented the space for twenty-five a night on the nights the club would be open—Thursday, Friday, and Saturday.

The concept behind the new club was that every college town needed a hot, smoky dive, someplace a little dangerous, barely legal, an improvised netherspace where students could go when they felt the need to seek the shadows. Curtis and Paul figured anyone who spent all night trying to find parties where their friends are, which was what the cool kids did, would pay a buck to get into a club where there are local bands and dancing and you know everybody there, where it was a dollar at the door and twenty-five cents for a beer in a small plastic cup.

At the time none of the clubs in Athens booked the new experimental original music, all classed as the generic punk/New Wave. Hippie music and cowboy music were better for the drinking crowd. Those more traditional bands were still getting the big weekend nights. Even at Tyrone's, which just that last summer had started booking some of the local bands, Pylon could only get Wednesday nights. New Wave didn't yet bring in spending crowds. None of the punk/New-Wavers drank at the bar. Nobody had any money. Instead they ordered water, danced, and drank under the tables from half pints hidden in brown paper bags.

Paul and Curtis got the place fixed up and they needed a name. First Scales said they should add an "e" to Crow and call it The Crowe's Nest, after Curtis Crowe. Curtis nixed that quick. Then he suggested they call it the 40 Watt Club, after the notorious party space just across the street where Curtis and Bill Tabor lived, the birthplace of Pylon, the site of great parties. At first Curtis didn't want to. He felt the 40 Watt Club was the name of the space whose time was done. But it was a good name and it did conjure up the low-budget image they were into. Curtis compromised. They named it The 40 Watt Club East.

They borrowed fifty dollars from Curtis' bandmate Vanessa, built the stage, painted the walls. They floated checks for the first night's beer and on May 20, 1980, Athens' first homemade new music rock club opened, the club whose name would become synonymous with the Athens music scene. It opened with The Side Effects, the band that had started the same night as R.E.M. at Kathleen's birthday party at the church a little more than a month earlier. A crowd packed the club. The Side Effects played what they called "bomp and stomp," a just sort of intent fun-rock with Kit the cute one playing guitar and singing and

Paul on drums, Jimmy on bass, both of them balding young and loving in their spare time the little girls.

At the end of the night Curtis and Paul saw that they'd made enough money to pay everybody what they owed, and even give some to the band.

They said, "Hey, this is easy!"

The punk/New Wave kids at last had their very own rock club. Soon R.E.M.'s Peter Buck and his girlfriend Ann Boyles, along with Ann's roommate Lisa Saylen, were in charge of the bar, selling cans of Bud or cups of Pabst. Peter and Ann had a system for the bar service: "You take all the guys," Peter told Ann. "And I'll take all the girls." On some nights, Linda Hopper and Michael Stipe filled in, following the same routine.

The 40 Watt East became the epicenter of the weekend nighttime downtown scene; the whole scene fit up there in the club, capacity about seventy-five. The kids went up there and got blasted outside themselves. They supped with the others on summer lightning and work-hate rage. For that few to many hours in the night they were transported from the college mill into a darkened club of their own, run by friends. During shows everyone danced pounding, and Curtis and Paul, every night during the three-night weekend run, went downstairs into the closed sandwich shop and wedged two-by-fours to brace the rafters and keep the floor from collapsing. The room had windows overlooking Broad Street and at night the kids from the club took over the streets below. They leaned from the windows and shouted at friends. They rolled down the long flight of stairs, wasted, working up bruises they would only discover the next day and wonder of their origin. One night that first summer someone brought a thermometer up there during an R.E.M. show and it topped a hundred and twenty-five degrees. That was normal. So between sets the kids milled around on the sidewalks along Broad Street and on North Campus, smoking joints under the trees and streetlights while the sweat steamed off their wet T-shirts and sticky clinging party dresses, and frat boys drove by six-to-their-Daddys' cars and threw beer cans and called them all faggots. The streets belonged to the kids. And when it got real late they were joined by weird East Georgia pillhead queens wearing dog collars and rouge, who came and sat on corner benches by the closed newsstand waiting for lovelorn friends. In addition the town's project-born transvestites, in thrift-store plether miniskirts hooked cruising rednecks who had driven their trucks into the *beeg ceetie* looking for the weekend action.

Everybody loved it. Nobody cared who did what. Nothing else mattered to the folk at the Watt except winning the Go-Go Contest and, after last call, when the plugs are pulled, leaving the club and sharing your victory prize—a plastic gallon jug of flat keg beer—with your gang on the street as you stumble on home.

19

R.E.M. PLAYS THEIR FIRST SHOW IN ATLANTA — MIKE MILLS IS LATE FOR AN INTERVIEW — R.E.M. GOES TO NORTH CAROLINA — A ROCK-AND-ROLL SICK THING

One night in June Sam and John Seawright were at a party in Athens when a woman wearing a man's suit came up to John and asked him if he wanted to go to Atlanta to hear some bands. John had taken his undergraduate degree at the university and had just returned from working on a masters at the University of Chicago. When the woman asked him if he wanted to go to Atlanta, he hesitated. He didn't know the woman; had never seen her before. But then she said she'd buy a case of beer. John found his brother Sam and said let's go.

They piled into the woman's big car. She pointed it west toward Atlanta and they took off. On the way out of town she stopped and bought a case of beer and a carton of wine. When she got back in the car she filled a plastic Bulldog to-go cup with the chablis, pulled a giant horse pill out of her purse, swallowed it, and headed for the show.

It was a three-act lineup at a downtown Atlanta warehouse.

148

On the bill was R.E.M., playing their first out-of-town show. Playing before them were The Space Heaters, an Atlanta band that played standard and fashionable New Wave covers, and Red Meat and Sprouts, a comedy troupe. The members of Red Meat and Sprouts that night got too drunk to perform well, and their act went unnoticed by the equally drunk crowd. Ironically, Red Meat and Sprouts took so long to fumble drunkenly through their alloted time that Peter Buck got pissed waiting for them to finish.

"*Fuck* them! *Fuck* them!" he repeatedly snarled, pacing.

Peter was nervous. And when Peter gets nervous Peter drinks beer, and by the time R.E.M. went on he too was thoroughly trashed, but that didn't effect his ability to chop through the dark, chop through the night, and play out his debut in his old hometown. The show that night was, by all reports, promising, but unremarkable. The local fanzine, *Useless Knowledge*, reported thus on their performance: "R.E.M. (Rapid Eye Movement) is another Athens band once again with that great sixties sound. This band does lots of covers, but does them well. Great for dancing and fun."

After the show at the warehouse ended, John and Sam looked for the woman who had driven them to Atlanta, but she was nowhere around. When they finally found her she was passed out in a stairwell, drooling vomit on her man's suit. They put her in the backseat, found the keys in her purse, and drove her car back to Athens. But just before they got into town they ran out of gas.

John and Sam flipped a coin to see who would walk to get gas. Sam lost. He left. John fell asleep in the front seat and the unknown woman still slept in the back. Before long John was awakened by a policeman's nightstick tapping on the window.

"Looks like you been having you-self a party," the cop said, shining the flashlight on the knocked-out, puke-stained woman in the backseat. "Whose car is this, anyway?"

"Uh, hers, officer," John said.

"What's your name, boy?"

"John Seawright, sir."

"Seawright? You related to Sam Seawright?"

"Uh, yes sir, he's my brother."

"Well, John, you in luck. I went to high school with Sam. You're okay for now, but you better be more careful in the future. We ran a check on this car, *and it don't come up registered nowhere!*"

Kathleen O'Brien, who by that time was steadily dating Bill Berry, had her own bad luck that night. She had driven her Satellite Sebring to Atlanta, hauling the ragged amps the band used at the time. After the show Bill disappeared somewhere and Kathleen was left to drive back to Athens alone, loaded down with amps and Bill's cymbals. Lucky for her. On the way out of Atlanta she was broadsided by a taxi, and the impact was absorbed by the band's equipment.

To round out the post-party misfortunes that night, Mike Mills and Mark Segura, a one-time member of the student senate at UGA and at that time a noted party dog and DJ at WUOG, fled from the warehouse after the show, went to the top of the Hyatt in Atlanta, drank ninety dollars worth of drinks, and played fast with the tab. Laughing, they ran out into the streets and stumbled through downtown. At one point they wandered near a police cordon on a blue-strobed avenue where a midnight sniper was holed up with hostages in a house. Mike and Mark blundered innocently close and the cops took one look at their red eyes and unsteady strides and threatened them with arrest just for being there: "Boys, you gettin' in our way!" By four A.M. the two were in a laundromat where a deranged bum threatened nobody, eyes pinball-rolling, saying to a wall, "I'm gunna cut you muthafuckin' haid off, *bwa.*"

Mike forgot that R.E.M. was scheduled to play in Athens the next night. Forgetting that, he also forgot that they had an interview on WUOG that afternoon. By three P.M. that next afternoon Michael, Peter, and Bill were in the radio station studio

on the top of Memorial Hall and were about to go on the air.
Mike still wasn't there. Finally he staggered in, bleary-eyed, wearing a brown and tan McDonald's hat. He had just ridden the
Greyhound bus back to Athens that morning. He had finally remembered the interview. But he forgot about the show. When
the rest of the band told Mike they had to play that night, he
just had one thing to say: "Ahg!"

At the end of the month the band finally moved out of the
church. It had served its purpose. Throughout that school year
it stood up to the repeated bombardment of beer bottles and
rock and roll. It provided shelter and ambience for endless parties. And most important, it had provided the stage for the debut
of R.E.M., the rising stars of the Athens scene. In that sense the
band felt a token nostalgia about the place, but not enough to
keep them there another year: The weather had turned hot, the
lousy carpet smelled of sour beer puke, and the fleas were already
nesting in everybody's hair: They couldn't wait to leave.

When they moved out of the church, Mike, Peter, and Michael sublet a house together from a couple of girls Michael
knew from the art school. Bill moved in with Kathleen in a house
just around the corner from the other three guys. It was very
convenient; the four guys saw each other almost every day, practicing and writing songs. Their band was new and young and
good. They thrilled at the thought of success to come. They
knew it was going to be a hot summer. They just didn't know
how hot.

In June, Pylon had decided they wanted to book some shows to
play along the road between New York and Athens. They could
use the dates to help cover expenses and earn a little extra rent
money. At the time however, mainstream clubs along the eastern
seaboard weren't interested in booking the new bands. In the
face of this resistance an underground circuit was beginning to
shape up: local bars with righteous cheek that booked these righ-

teous bands. Vic Varney, who was both playing in The Method
Actors and booking Pylon, heard about Chapel Hill, a little North
Carolina college town much like Athens, and how it too had a
couple of clubs willing to take the risk with original rock. He
talked to some folks: got a name to call: Jefferson Holt.

Jefferson worked at a record store along Franklin Street in
Chapel Hill. Franklin Street was the main drag in that college
town where everybody went to buy records and so, like Pete
Buck in Athens and Danny Beard in Atlanta, Jefferson met all
the musicians and the club owners. Like musicians everywhere,
they all hung out at the record stores talking about shit.

"Just like in Athens, there weren't places for the new bands
to play," Holt recalled ten years later. "The clubs weren't booking them. But for me, I knew the guys who were in bands and
the guys who ran the clubs. So I made use of what I had and I
talked the clubs into booking bands. But it was all in play. My
roommate and I were into doing stuff, like, we made up a band
that never played but got written up in some fanzines. The band
was called WASP—White Anglo-Saxon Punks. Pretty stupid, I
know. And also, since I was helping bands get booked, we made
up a production company. We made signs and gave it a name
and everything. We called it Dasht Hopes Productions.

"So one day I got a phone call from Vic, who was managing
Pylon. I didn't know Vic. I had never met any of Pylon. I hadn't
even really *heard* of them! But I imagined they were doing the
same thing as up here. Nobody knew what a manager was, nobody knew what a promoter was, nobody knew what being in a
band was, and everybody was just having a blast partying and
wanted to make something happen so you could keep having
fun and not have to get a real job.

"And Vic calls me and says, 'I manage Pylon, we need a
date going to New York.' "

Jefferson says sure, he'll get them a date. Then Vic calls up
later and says Pylon can't make it but The Method Actors will
do it. Jefferson says okay again. Then, as the date got close, Vic

canceled The Method Actors and Jefferson was stuck for a band. He asked Vic if there was anyone else who could play and Vic mentioned a few of the new bands in Athens and suggested, "Maybe try one of them." A friend of Jefferson's had recently visited Athens and he asked her who he should get. She uttered these fateful words to the man who would become their manager: "Get R.E.M. They're better than anybody else."

Vic gave Bill Berry a number and Bill called Jefferson, who that day was sick in bed with fever. Jefferson could barely hold the receiver but he wheezed a confirmation: the last weekend in July, two weekend nights in Chapel Hill and a Monday in Raleigh.

It was to be R.E.M.'s first night out of Georgia. When they got the date they decided that since they had never been on the road before, they were going to go for it. All four of the guys had, since their early teen dreaming days, embedded the roadtrip schema in their collective unconscious from repeated reading of paperback rock-and-roll biographies: What do you do when you're in a band on the road? Stay drunk, bed women, never sleep, never eat. And like a subliminal program keyed to the sound of wheels on asphalt, when R.E.M. hit the road that first time and for the many times through the next many years, the legend rose up to consume them, and true to their badly longed-for rock-and-roll vision, R.E.M. that weekend in North Carolina stayed drunk, never ate, and never slept, unless it was next to someone stray-fetched and bar-met:

R.E.M. drove to Chapel Hill and pulled into Franklin Street, found Jefferson, and got directions to the club. That night they played at The Station. Michael ate a Quaalude, which was like speed to him, and that and a few beers and Pete's Rickenbacker kick and Mike and Bill's rhythms turned him into his special and amazing wind-curled liquid smoke. This band was from Athens, and they might have that fun sixties sound, but they were nothing like the loopy B-52's, nothing like the machine-tight Pylon. Playing their songs about girls and cars, R.E.M. was fast, sloppy, dude rock. Stipe whipped himself loose-jointed and throat-choking across the stage, off it, into the audience, on top of the bar. Stipe and the beer and dope together rent his shirt and stained it with sweat, knotted his wet curling bangs and glazed his eyes and sent a convincing signal note through the country-side that from then on out R. fucking E. fucking M. was going to blast hell out of the 1980s rock-and-roll scene.

While the band played, tearing out their set, the audience watched, curious, eyes a-bug, mouths agape, tongues a-hanging. There was definitely something about these guys. And while they played and the audience stared, a big car with a crushed driver's door and Georgia plates pulled up outside. Inside the car were Kathleen O'Brien, Linda Hopper, and Leslie Michel: R.E.M.'s first self-declared groupies, ready to rock.

"We went up there innocently enough," Leslie Michel says. Leslie was also an Effectette, a go-go dancer with The Side Effects. "The band didn't know we were coming, and me and Hopper and Kathleen drove up in Kathleen's Satellite, which still had its bashed-in side from the Atlanta show, and we had to get in and out on the passengers' side. We rented this real cheesy room and had all this liquor and the only reason we could go was 'cause I put all the gas on my credit card. We rented this hotel room and it was like a real rock-and-roll sick thing. Nobody knew who we were and we had this huge party, tearing down the motel.

"Anyway, Jefferson and David Healy were doing the door and they weren't going to let us in because they didn't know us, but we just walked past them and started dancing. We jumped up on the bar and we flipped everyone out because when the band saw us they all screamed and jumped, missed notes and everything, and all of us were dancing and got the whole place all whipped up.

"That was where David Healy and Jefferson came into our lives."

"The next day we went to an A-frame on a lake where Jefferson was running around in his underwear," remembers Linda

Hopper. "Michael and I were looking at this book of pornography through the ages that Jefferson had, just watching him, saying, 'God, who *is* this guy in the black underwear?' We were there for a couple days and slept at David Healy's girlfriend's apartment, and we went swimming and we would go in the pool and all of us were in T-shirts sticking to us. It was Jefferson's birthday party. We went to all of their out-of-town shows."

"The fallout after the show," Jefferson remembers, "was that everybody who was in a band hated them because Peter only knew three chords. But a lot of people liked them because of their energy. The band stayed up all night and ended up in the pool at Healy's. We had a birthday party for me on Sunday. And on Monday they went to Raleigh and there was nobody there. Nobody was up front where the band was, they were back in the dark, watching. As soon as they started playing Healy and I went out and grabbed chairs and were dancing with chairs. By the end of the show the band was completely off-stage and the audience was onstage."

After the shows Jefferson said to the band, "You guys are great. You're the best band I've ever seen. You're like The Who or something."

The next month, Jefferson and Healy got directions to R.E.M.'s studio in Athens and came down for a visit. It was summertime and the streets were empty. They didn't know how to get to the band's Jackson Street studio but they heard the sound of music and followed it to the source. They met up with the band. By the end of their first day in town they found themselves at a party at a house where Pylon's Michael Lachowski lived called Pylon Park. Yet another new Athens band was debuting. This one was called Love Tractor.

20

"SOMETHING IS HAPPENING IN ATHENS" — THE POST-BOUFFANT BOP — PYLON PARK — LOVE TRACTOR DEBUTS

Something is happening in Athens. . . ." the *New York Rocker* declared in its July/August 1980 issue. In the wake of The B-52's success with their first album, enhanced and confirmed and nationally spread after an appearance on *Saturday Night Live,* the new music press turned the spotlight on the little Georgia college town and looked in wonder at the place that had produced one of Warner Bros. hottest acts, as well as the two new bands that were killing them in New York, Pylon and The Method Actors.

The writer of the *New York Rocker* article ended his paean to this fecund little miracle lab with an invitation to any readers ready to find a site for adventure in rock:

"Athens is full of empty buildings, cheaply rented, where bands can rehearse without noise complaints. Try tuning your guitar to EADGGD or EADGBB or EECGDA! Go south and create a scene! And remember: If you're going to Athens, Georgia, be sure to wear a beehive in your hair."

Of course, no one would wear a beehive in their hair in Athens in the summer of 1980. That was The B-52's style, and they were gone. Their drag street theater was a thing of the past, their wigs already sanctified and quickly becoming clichéd themselves. Even Jerry Ayers, Keith Strickland's and Ricky Wilson's praised and touted influence, had given up drag and was developing a new bohemian hay-cuff ragman style, taking Michael Stipe under his wing.

Pylon guitarist Randy Bewley did use unconventional tunings, as did Ricky Wilson, but in contrast to the symphony of cultural refuse that the B's put forward, Pylon was clean and minimal. Vic Varney, playing guitar in the two-man ensemble of The Method Actors, also used odd tunings to create a barrage of noise to make up for the lack of a bass guitar or keyboards, but The Method Actors' sound was muscular and aggressive, propelled by the he-man image and muscular pounding of drummer David Gamble.

Neither of those two Athens bands was loopy and boppy like The B-52's, but they each scored in New York City, getting gigs through club impresario Jim Fouratt and causing everyone to monitor developments in Athens. The British paper *New Musical Express* declared that, "aprés The B-52's" Athens was "still weird, but definitely not wacky." They called it the "Post-Bouffant Bop."

The Post-Bouffant Bop was headquartered at the house on Barber Street where Michael Lachowski and Randy Bewley lived. The driveway led from Barber in a steep, flagstoned rut, up the bluff along which the houses on that side of the street stood, up and into the gravel and dirt parking lot—then out again the back way, along another dirt alley cut through a bamboo thicket. The back parking lot was a place for parties, where Michael Lachowski strung lights, ran speakers in the brush and up the trees. As it was the headquarters and party site for Lachowski's band it was duly named, house and yard, Pylon Park.

One time that summer there was a party there that was just

a party, and it went for a while and it got late and after midnight there was a TV Bash. A guy got up on the roof of the house with a TV set that was plugged into a long extension cord, some late show flickering on screen, and he lifted it above his head and shouted, "*Fuck* TV!" And everybody shouted in response, "*Fuck* TV! Yeah! *Fuck* TV!" Then the guy threw the TV off the house and it exploded. And all of a sudden these other guys ran up and doused the TV with gasoline and set it on fire and everybody went crazy, shouting, "Yeah, *Fuck* TV! *Fuck* TV!" And the TV was burning and for about three minutes it was really cool. "*Fuck* TV! *Fuck* TV!" But then this huge black cloud of toxic smoke shifted. Instead of going straight up in the air it started hovering and moving around at ground level, this huge noxious black cloud, and everybody ran away. That was the end of that party.

The night Jefferson Holt came to Athens with his friend David Healy, a new friend, Ingrid Schorr, took them to a party at Pylon Park.

In the foyer of the house Love Tractor set up for their debut.

Love Tractor was made up of Mark Cline and Mike Richmond on guitar, with Kit Swarz on drums. Kit was playing with The Side Effects, but since he was neighbors to Mark Cline there at Pylon Park he found it easy to play with them, too.

It was July 9, 1980, and Love Tractor set up in the foyer and played their six songs over and over again while the party went on and spread through the house, out the back porch to the packed-dirt parking lot and the thick hedges, old oaks and bamboo. The party had kegs of beer and everyone was there. When the kegs were emptied, Sam Seawright, who had roadied with Cline for The Tone Tones, brought out a tub of green homemade beer and the party kept on. Before the night was out Method Actors drummer David Gamble wrestled Pylon singer Vanessa Briscoe to the ground. To apologize, he drank some of Sam's homemade beer out of Vanessa's sweaty, gritty jelly shoe.

When that didn't quench his thirst he lifted the trash tub and drained the dregs.

Prior to that summer most student bands played jazz fusion, or blues, or covers of rock. But Love Tractor played "existential Ventures meets the Cure" instrumentals. When brainstorming their style they decided not to have lyrics, because a PA was too expensive and too hard to haul around. With that move, the courage to go strictly instrumental, they were quickly the darlings of the art school sect. Immediately they went from parties to the clubs, entering the cabal of bands like Pylon, The Side Effects, R.E.M. By the end of the summer Armstead Wellford had joined Love Tractor playing bass, and through Mark Cline's connections with The B-52's they began to get some dates in New York City. Since Kit Swarz played in both Love Tractor and The Side Effects, he wrangled The Side Effects a New York date as well.

Of that year's original newpunk Athens bands, only R.E.M. had not yet played New York. They preferred to wait a while. Despite the artsy charm of Love Tractor and the boppy fun of The Side Effects, R.E.M. was undoubtedly the best in Athens. No matter the cachet of a New York date, they didn't need it. Already they impressed everyone who saw them. They didn't want to get a one-night stand in New York and fool themselves into thinking that made them stars. They wanted a reputation built on solid ground. They wanted there to be no doubts. They wanted to dominate.

"This is the band that plays rock 'n' roll that sounds very familiar," wrote a reviewer in the Atlanta fanzine *Useless Knowledge* after R.E.M. played the 688 Club there in July. "This band plays rock 'n' roll songs that are covers, and plays songs that are not covers, and plays songs that are not covers that sound like covers. But it all sounds familiar and it is all danceable. And tonight we all danced to this familiar sound."

21

THE MAKE ME DANCE HOUSE — BARBER STREET — R.E.M. HEADQUARTERS — THE STREET OF STARS

In late summer, 1980, a clutch of archaeology students moved into a house on Meigs Street. On the front porch they discovered, nailed to a post, a little toy diorama in which a three-inch woman stood on a small stage under a plastic carnival tent. The little woman held her hands behind her head and she arched her back, presenting her tasseled breasts. At the bottom of the box was a crank: Turn the crank and the woman undulates as a wire inside turns. Repeated use had torn the woman's weathered rubber belly. But despite the tear the woman went on grinding as the crank was turned and the rusty gear poked out with each revolution, like a gruesome intestinal parasite, slowly widening the slit. On the post above the novelty toy the house's nickname was written in black Magic Marker: The Make Me Dance House.

The house was like many in the Cobbham and Normaltown student districts, all humbled by decay. The shiver-grip of winter and the expansive heat of summer alternately shrunk and swole clapboards till they popped nails and fell like sheets of old bark from pine beetle-bit dead trees, leaving the houses looking unrepaired, rough. The yards were bare dirt, tree-rooted, or weed-thick shoulder-high. The rooms were cheap.

Inside The Make Me Dance House the windows rattled and the plaster in the walls was crumbling to its original horsehair and mud dust. In the bathroom the curling linoleum was slippery with mildew, the floorboards moist and slowly rotting around the old porcelain toilet and sink that had been rigged by some distant white-trash tenants. In deep summer flies found their fun in that slip and slime, and slugs crawled up on the cool sweating pipes. The walls of the kitchen were painted slut-red. Broken furniture and the body-greased pallets of hippies past junked the rooms.

While cleaning out the house the archaeology students, alert to what they excavated, discovered, hidden in a hole in a bedroom floor, down in the under-house cold-dirt crawl space, a chipped concrete statue of St. Francis of Assisi with multi-colored candle wax dripped on his head, his mouth chipped oval by chisel and pick. The statue was wrapped in a gargantuan brassiere stained with red mud and ink and was buried in a waterlogged heap of pornographic magazines. In the bedroom closet they found red-ink diaries written in code and Ken dolls dressed up in Barbie's drag. Wondering what had gone on there, they looked for clues. They asked around.

Some held that The B-52's had once lived there.

Turned out it was only Fred Schneider, although it was only rumor that connected him to the stuff they found.

It was just over one year since The B-52's had signed their contract with Warner Bros., and already they were gone and barely remembered as having lived in town. Memory is short in a college town, and past tracks are quickly kicked up and clod over by the constant trek of new students coming to town, tramping through the streets looking for rooms to rent. All that was left of "the first Athens band" was rubbish and rumors. The B's were gone, already legend. But in their place had come up a new set of bands, Pylon and The Method Actors, proving that there was something peculiar about Athens, some intangible quality that nobody could figure. And what those first bands promised, the second wave—R.E.M., Love Tractor, The Side Effects—confirmed: Athens might be just a little hick college town hosting a handful of kids feeding on each other's energy, but it finally and certainly qualified as a scene. The 40 Watt Club was open, rent was cheap, and a student loan was enough to get you by, supplemented by a part-time job slicing weenies at a steak house salad bar, selling used records, or running photocopy machines. Or, like Ingrid Schorr, selling peeks at her pointy bra for twenty-five cents each.

Everyone was an artist and could do anything they wanted. They lived in a pretty little Dixie town where in first spring daffodils grew and, in summer, bachelor's buttons; when the sun was out, tripping young girls with grass seed stuck to the dew on their calves picked armfuls of flowers and carried them house to house in old coffee cans, escorted along the cracked sidewalks by scarecrow poets who made love to men. When hot, they could drive five miles out and find a lake where rednecks never go, where it was cool and okay to hang your clothes on the branches of trees, swim naked at night and have sex al fresco, streaked with mud and sweat, leaving the tall grass soft and broken.

These kids, a collection of high school outcasts and precocious talents, felt pretty good about themselves. Athens was like a rock opera version of *Lord of the Flies* meets *Gilligan's Island,* where the twenty-one-year-olds can't believe they are no longer twelve. They're all stranded on a deserted island, but their checks from home still come in the mail. Each day brought a new adventure: Gilligan got lost, the Skipper went crazy, headhunters from New York City came to town and everybody got scared, only to laugh in the end and pose for the cameras. Like the island in Golding's novel about children gone savage, Athens had its hunters, too, but these chased pork of a different kind—and they hunted for it at bars and parties, cafes and the corner cookie store.

And when they scored, the hunters returned triumphantly grease-stained to the place that served them that season as haven and council ring: the rambling and majestic house at 169 Barber Street. . . .

At one time, the view from that house at 169 Barber was a vista of homes and yards and quietude, but by 1980 the view included a convenience store, a car wash, and the grocery store loading dock. But it was still a glorious home. Barber Street was much grander than Meigs, and the house at 169 was the grandest of all.

Barber Street itself was just a short strip of road. At one end a Majik Market and a grocery store. At the other end the street changed its name, plunged downhill, and went on north out of Athens through black neighborhoods to where the white trash lived, where the yards were packed dirt and flowers, and chickens pecked along the cinderblock foundations of the old clapboard company homes. But in that two hundred yards of Barber Street proper, between the stoplight at the corner and the crest of the hill, in what was once a nice neighborhood, the renegade New Wavers set up and rigged their Left Bank community. In the rented high-ceilinged rooms just a ten-minute walk from the campus, folk in new rock bands were living out their art.

One sixty-nine became the center of the scene after Linda Hopper and Leslie Michel moved in. Linda, who had lived in the subbasement of Reed Hall and the D Phi U house on the highway, had been living during the summer in a house on Meigs, which she loathed; The Salvation Army shelter for slack-eyed and hair-faced drifters was only a half block away. One day she was walking the streets depressed, and as she turned down Barber she saw a friend from high school sitting at the top of a set of steps that climbed the bluff from the street to the sprawling porch at 169. Her friend, Larry Marcus, who would play keyboards in The Little Tigers with Paul Lombard, another popular Athens band, lived at the house. Larry told Linda that the hippies downstairs were moving out.

They looked inside the vacant apartment and Linda saw that the paint might be peeling, but at least the walls weren't crumbling and the hardwood floors were fitted and braced. There were wooden mantles over the old coal fireplaces and huge sliding doors that opened between rooms where the ceilings were thirteen feet high and voices echoed even when they weren't empty.

She got a number from Larry and went across the street to the public pay phone bolted to the outside wall of the Majik Market. Her hands trembling with anticipation, she called the landlord and got the house.

Linda moved into the house along with Leslie Michel, the horticulture major slash party babe who had led the raid on Chapel Hill earlier in the summer when R.E.M. played their first out-of-state gig. Leslie was the kind of invaluable party mistress all scenes need, the kind who would hustle a hat and take up collections for a beer resupply run when parties got too crowded and the kegs drained too quickly. Linda and Leslie invited Mark Phredd Rizzo to join them at 169. Mark Phredd was a big boy, a gay Catholic kid with a mother fixation, who would later become well known in Manhattan's club scene for his Mr. Hapi Phace act at the Pyramid Club.

Mark Phredd and the girls moved in and set up in the open rooms. The walls and mantles, the porch and windows, were of the pure and stately honorable quality that welcomed and gave grace to any display of reliquary. Sheers dug from the rag room of Potter's House hung draped like webs from tacks in the window frames. The beds were layered with blankets unmatched in design, luxurious in their variety and clean warmth of natural fibers. The mantle garniture was an ever-varying set of iconographic detritus: plastic Christs, candles, broken mirrors, snapshot Polaroids and Barbie dolls, broken records and animal bones.

As the girls occupied 169, the R.E.M. boys—Peter, Michael,

and Mike—moved out of their summer sublet, leaving it wrecked and scarred. They followed the movement of the scene to Barber Street. Peter and his girlfriend Ann moved into a house near 169. Mike and his girlfriend Lauren moved in next door. Michael stashed his clothes at his parents' house in the country and took to crashing on the floor with Linda at 169 itself until he moved into an apartment there with Mike Huff, where the two of them subsisted that winter on potato quiches. Bill and Kathleen stayed where they were on the edge of town, but soon began spending most of their time on Barber Street with the rest of the crowd.

And the crowd was big, and getting bigger. Upstairs at 169, guitarist Paul Lombard and Larry Marcus were writing songs for The Little Tigers. Pylon Park, which was only a half-dozen houses down Barber Street from 169, was already serving as a primary party site. Members of Pylon, Love Tractor, and The Side Effects lived there, and all around them, on nearby alleys, came and nested the ever-fluxing cast of itinerant students and artists, scenemakers all.

At 169, they lived in their playground. Nineteen-eighty to 1981 was a hot time, and with Michael Stipe's oncoming fame, they all couldn't help but laugh as the girls and Mark Phredd pulled up his shirt and drew on his flat belly. Linda, Leslie, Mark Phredd, Michael, and Carol Levy, whom Michael had met the year before at the church when he smeared lip gloss into her face, spent many gin-soaked afternoons reading out loud from *Celebrity Skin*, junk-store pornography Michael had found, or the *Penthouse* "Forum," all of them bemoaning the plight of the flaccid penis.

Bored with that, someone would shout, "Let's play the game!" and, shrieking, they grabbed someone to serve as a victim and tied them up, tickling them until they passed out . . . then they tied up someone else. Or Mark Phredd would shout "Sexercise!" and they'd put on records to dance, Mark Phredd choreographing the scene with his call and response: "Who are we?" "We're the Mark Phredd Dancers!" "What do we do?" "We dance!" "And how do we do it?" "Hard!" And Mark Phredd would go, clap clap, "Come on, Mommies! Sexercise!" And Michael Stipe couldn't help but laugh.

When they left the house to go shopping they often did their routine they called "The Loud Family," after a public television series. As the Loud Family Leslie Michel was Elvira, Linda was Sheila, Mark Phredd was Audy, and Michael Stipe was Shep. In stores they shouted from aisle to aisle, "Hey Shep! Where's da Hershey's Syrup! *I need my Hershey's Syrup!*" And through the streets the New York/New Jersey accents of the Loud Family echoed, irritating to no end almost everybody who heard the routine.

But it was the partying that was the season's essence: Leslie Michel would finish washing dishes and then call The Party Line, Michael Lachowski's answering machine which he had turned over as a public service to be the clearinghouse for party information. Leslie would record the message "Scotch party at 169!" and in ten minutes the sidewalks were alive with people coming over with flasks in hand and dance shoes on their feet—all rockers with a mission and an unquenchable thirst. Parties in all those houses along Barber Street that season just happened. A gang would spark up and everyone would all drink as much as they could and dope up and after an all-night freak of witty conversation they would fall silent, the last bottle dry, the last baggy licked, and it would be six A.M. and they would be sitting around in a circle, smoking filterless cigarettes and blinking the sun from their eyes. One time, Leslie got so dogsick at a party that she was in bed for a week and Michael Stipe kept coming in and holding a mirror to her mouth to make sure she was still breathing.

Eventually, even Jefferson Holt migrated from North Carolina to Athens. He came in October 1980 to run a record store for a friend, but after the store closed he stuck around. In spring 1981 the twenty-seven-year-old moved into 169 across the foyer from Linda and Leslie, taking over Michael Stipe's apartment,

Michael's bedroom becoming the band's practice room after they quit their Jackson Street studio. Once in town to stay, Jefferson immediately plunged into the frenetic, hallucinatory party scene that came to be associated with Barber Street, the most prestigious address of the Golden Age of the Athens music scene. So notable had the registry of that street become that one night in early fall two of the town's finest party babes wrote its status in cement:

Maureen McLaughlin, the B's ex-manager, and Vanessa Briscoe, Pylon's singer, one night were walking down Barber Street, heading to a daiquiri party at 169. Pylon's first album, *Gyrate*, had come out in October to rave reviews, and they were planning to go to England before Christmas. Maureen and Vanessa saw where the city had just patched a square in the sidewalk and the cement was still wet. Balancing their cocktails, they fell to their knees and, squealing with the thrill of vandalism, scratched with their fingers in the wet cement the names of the street's best-known residents: Pylon, R.E.M., The Side Effects, Love Tractor, The Swindles. Spilling rum on their work, they christened Barber with the nickname that would stick for years in the cement as well as in local legend:

The Street of Stars.

22

THE MEN'S CLUB — A FRESH SEASON IN ATHENS — R.E.M. RAIDS THE COUNTRYSIDE — R.E.M. RECORDS A SINGLE

It was summer; the air was wet and sticky. The humidity that had oppressed the afternoon was beginning to lessen, but it was still high enough that the cigar smoke that rolled from the ends of a dozen thumb-fat Swisher Sweets was kept together in thick, gray ribbons as the meeting of the Men's Club was called to disorder.

The announcement for a meeting had gone out the day before: "Men's Club at Bill and Mike's." Bill Berry and Mike Mills, best friends since high school in Macon, and now the double-punch power pack driving R.E.M., had recently moved in together to a house on Barber Street next door to Pylon Park. They figured it was their turn to host a party. They declared a Men's Club meeting, and after six o'clock the members began showing up: Curtis Crowe and Michael Lachowski from Pylon; Nicky Giannaris from the defunct Tone Tones; the painter Neil MacArthur; Love Tractor manager Glen Chitlik; the party favorites brothers Sam and John Seawright—and many more of the men of the scene trouped into Bill and Mike's house, popped beers, lit up their cigars, and launched into an experience of male bonding that was only slightly belied by the layer of parody that glossed the proceedings.

As the crowd grew, the cloud of smoke thickened and the dirty jokes became raunchier. A topless waitress, someone's willing girlfriend (and the only woman allowed), shook her small breasts and served beer from a tray. The sun wasn't down before the shells from the boiled peanuts, the traditional Men's Club snack, were ankle-deep on the floor, five cases of beer had been emptied, and two packs of Polaroid film had been used up shooting guy-pics of mooning butts and beery mugging. Eying the pile of empty beer bottles, Bill Berry pulled out his golf clubs and he and Curtis Crowe took turns standing on the kitchen table, smashing the empty bottles with the clubs, one spotting for the other—"You do a case then ah'll do one!"—while Mike Mills tugged his baseball cap down tighter and laughed hysterically against the rain of glass. The bottles shattered with an exquisite noise, and for a year after there was glass in the cupboards and shining slivers stuck to the walls. After it got dark Sandi Phipps, Kathleen O'Brien, and a couple of other girls tried to crash the party but the men wrestled them to the floor, threw them down the front porch steps, and hurled full cans of beer after them, barely missing their heads and putting still more dents in Kathleen's already battered Plymouth Satellite.

It was a new summer, another fresh season in Athens, Gee-A. That past December, a writer in England's *New Musical Express* had reviewed Pylon's album *Gyrate*, calling it "one of the year's most fundamental rock-and-roll celebrations." Another writer raised the issue of geography that was on everyone's mind: "Without trying to hype Athens, Georgia, into a new Akron, Ohio, it's fair to say that the success of The B-52's has had a great effect on the young natives of that quiet college town. . . .

Pylon are southern kids, from small towns in Georgia and Florida. They have that slow drawl, that take-things-easy attitude. A 'Gosh, are we really in the music business now?' innocence that still registers on their faces and still rings true. . . ."

In January of 1981 *Melody Maker* also reviewed Pylon and noted that "buried deep in the land of rednecks, peanut farms and wave-yer-hat-and-shout-yeehaw boogie bands, there's something stirring."

And just on the newsstands as summer began was an issue of the *New York Rocker* with Pylon on the cover. Inside was a feature spread on Athens. It was validation: "New Sounds from the New South" the headline blared. Pylon was the lead, with a second feature on The Method Actors. A summary tribute written by Vic Varney was also included: "Athens: Small Town Makes Good." And as a wrap-up, photos of the three youngest bands: R.E.M., Love Tractor, and The Side Effects. Vic said about R.E.M.: "Except for the B's, they could probably pack in more people on a given night than any band around." With that as their reputation, R.E.M. began to think about cutting a single.

The residents of Barber Street—Pylon, Love Tractor, R.E.M.—felt themselves to be quite the items as 1981 fleshed itself out and enhanced the steadily growing reputation of Athens. Ronald Reagan had just been elected and a new wave of conservatism was cranked and rolling in America. With that shadow of Reaganism falling over the country, the artistes and fine young party things in Athens felt themselves to be even more precious because of their rejection of it. They were the privileged post-punk retainers of a classic Baudelairian decadence in the face of the new repression. They were late twentieth-century members of the cult of multiplied sensation.

The most spectacular event that spring was the Easter party at 169. Invitations went out and Leslie Michel wrote risky checks all over town to scrounge enough fruit and liquor to make a tub of punch. The lion-clawed bathtub was moved to the front porch and a 3-D Christ was hung above it. The yard filled with the folks in Easter finery who showed up, filled a cup, and had a hit of blotter laid on their tongues. The trigger to kick occurred when David Helmey drove up. He got his invitation to the party, but he thought it was a costume ball. He rode up on his Honda 750. He was wrapped in a sheet, his long red hair kept in place by a crown of woven kudzu. As he walked up the long flight of stairs, the bunch on the porch began to yell and clap. When he reached the top Leslie laid a dose on his tongue and the party shifted gears.

As the stereo speakers in the window alternated Gershwin with The Gang of Four, John Seawright sat hunched on the porch swing, flanked by admiring babes. He smoked his Camels down to the thick orange callus on his fingers while he lulled the girls into a mystic torpor with his profound voice, telling them of the finer points of Gnostic Manichaeanism. Linda, Leslie, and the other girls twirled in the yard and sucked fruit from their cups. Paul Lombard ambled in and out of the foyer, mumbling, serving sips of punch to his little cat Trotsky. Jefferson laughed about a recurring dream involving Minnie and Mickey Mouse. And Gene-Gene the dancing machine, a short black mechanic from town, stumbled through the crowd, offering his assistance to the girls. Before the Easter party was over Gene-Gene had fallen asleep in an old overstuffed chair that had been hauled onto the porch.

He missed it when Peter Buck washed Leslie's feet in the dregs of the grain punch and then drank it.

To the rest of the town's standard students, however, Barber Street and its residents had a different reputation than that of bohemian artists, the one imagined for themselves. Because of their difference—their costume, hair color and cut—they were seen as both dangerous and ridiculous. They were called "that Barber Street crowd": offbeat costuming bohos, self-righteous New Wave trendies who fancied themselves somehow more blessed than average, asshole henna-heads who thought a ragged linen slip, oversized woolen pants, and a pack-a-day Camel habit made them better than anyone else. But while the other students might sneer, they were at the same time enthralled.

At 169, Leslie and Linda had the walls of one open and sunny room lined with their favorite black party dresses—black satin, black polyester, black cotton, black rayon bodice, and huge black polka dots on a full skirt—and at some party, who knows which, some frat kids wandered in, attracted by the smell and sounds of a party at night, and they saw the dancing and drinking, the girls lifting their dresses over their heads, the boys touching boys, the dismembered mannequins painted with lipstick. Confused and worried, they left to tell their friends.

What they said must not have been good. In the retelling, the party dresses that had been pulled from the piles in Potter's House thrift-store ragroom, became satanic robes donned by both sexes during wild rockannalias. The dancing kids, refracted in a drunk frat boy's mind, became lupine sex fiends, mad from drugs and punk. The stories that were passed around on campus about the rockers on Barber Street only enhanced the intrigue. Soon it became a standard frat dare to challenge a pledge to go to Barber, climb the long sets of stairs to the wide deep porch of 169, look in the windows, knock on the doors, and then run away.

Nobody ever took the dare, or else nobody ever noticed. But it would have been easy. The house was party central in a scene known for partying; people came and went at all hours. The crowd that lived along Barber Street was a very partying crowd. Time was marked by the passage of parties and time was also obliterated by the same, each episode adding a scar to someone's body or reputation, to be retold by others over beers.

At this time all the members of R.E.M. were living on Barber Street and practicing in a room at 169. They were writing two new songs each week: rock-thrash-verse-chorus-bridge. It was what Michael would later consider their "songwriting apprenticeship," during which time they practiced five days a week. Everything was perfect: They were writing plenty of songs, packing the clubs, getting press, and they had even just recently added a fifth member to their organization: their new manager, Jefferson Holt:

Until they added Jefferson Bill Berry had done all of the booking for R.E.M., with some help from his girlfriend Kathleen. At the same time Bill also had taken on double duty as drummer for Love Tractor as well, after Kit Swarz decided to devote all his time to school and The Side Effects. Bill was ambitious, energetic, and willing to do anything, but the load of playing with two bands and managing one began to wear on him. Every day after practicing with R.E.M. he went over to Kathleen's and spent the evening complaining that nobody else in the band wanted to help deal with the business. Everybody wanted to make money playing music—they'd all committed themselves to that—but they bitched when the phone calls and bank deposits had to be made. Finally he came to a breaking point. Bill couldn't handle the pressure alone, so the four members of R.E.M. decided they needed a fifth.

The time was right. Bill had put together a string of dates for April 1981, where the band traveled steadily from Georgia to Tennessee to North Carolina and around again in twelve days. It was to be their first extended tour longer than a weekend. Jefferson Holt had proven himself to be a loyal fan and a stout partyer since he'd moved into 169 Barber Street, plus he had some experience dealing with club owners. When R.E.M. decided to recruit a road hand, they thought of him.

Jefferson was visiting his old friends in Chapel Hill when Bill gave him a call. It was nothing firm, Bill explained, but he wanted to know if Jefferson could go on tour with them to help load equipment, take money at the door. Jefferson jumped at the chance, said, "Hell yeah!" He got in his car and drove to Athens.

"I drove down and got to the studio on Jackson Street just as they were finishing loading," Jefferson remembers. "All the girls were there and everybody was waiting for me. I had been visiting a friend of mine who's a painter and I had shaved my head to pose for a series of paintings he was doing. Plus, I'd planned on going to an Easter party as an egg. So I get out of the car with my head shaved and wearing a smoking jacket and everybody just stared at me. They were horrified. But Bill said, 'Get in. Let's go!' and I crawled into the back of their old green van and I've never left."

A few days later, at a party after the show in Chapel Hill, Jefferson and the members of the band were standing around outside. "That was when Bill came up to me and asked if I wanted to manage the band," Jefferson says. "See, with them, everybody was broke and the band's money belonged to everybody, so whoever had control of the money eventually pissed off everybody else. But I could say no to somebody and have it not disrupt the band itself. I could be the whipping boy and Mr. Moneybags at the same time. So when Bill asked me, I said yes."

The relationship between Jefferson and the band got off to a slippery start. Before he had been asked to help manage the band, Jefferson made up some posters that said "Rapid Eye Movement, Spring Tour '81." The band hated that, and Michael Stipe especially was furious. "By that time Michael had gone on his hate-rapid-eye-movement kick, but I didn't know," Jefferson says. "I was just trying to help out."

Michael Stipe was more than the band's singer/songwriter. He was its image consultant and creative director. He had always been aware of style and image, but his sense of it became even stronger once he got deeper into his study of art and his band began to get popular. The first step he took was to carefully bury any living memory of his playing in the band Gangster under the name Michael Valentine. In nearly every interview R.E.M. became his first band, although he sometimes vaguely acknowledged his high school experience.

He also carefully amended his taste in music and art. For example: One time, Michael and Linda Hopper went to Potter's

House to shop. Linda found a large wax candle there, hand-carved with the names of bands: Boston, Aerosmith, ELO. She thought it was cute. She showed it to Michael but he didn't say anything. A few days later she came home to Barber Street and found Michael scraping the candle with a knife, obliterating the band names. "What are you doing?" Linda asked him. "Linda, this candle used to be mine. I made it when I was in high school. *My mother must have given it away!"*

The second step was to make clear that the name R.E.M., as used by them, did not stand for that stage during sleep when dreaming is its most intense, although that meaning was crucial to the early rocking neo-beat surrealist image of the band. By declaring that the meaning of the name R.E.M. was open for interpretation Michael gracefully evaded the "rapid eye movement" stigma, and equated the experience of R.E.M. with dreaming itself.

Michael's personal image was equally vague. As he discovered artistic movements he tried them on, felt their fit: Dada, surrealism, expressionism; Rimbaud, Verlaine, Burroughs. During the early days he tried it all. Resisting the discipline of school, Michael and his friends skipped their classes at the university to drink gin-and-tonic in the overgrown yards along Barber Street and make messes on their bedroom floors with watercolors and cigarette ash. In Linda Hopper's bedroom at 169 Barber Michael set up a Farfisa which he'd bought from the wife of a local musician, cleaned it of the roaches he found nesting there, got the wiring repaired, and attempted to learn the instrument. This was his practice: Turn on the tape recorder, stick popsicle sticks between a couple of randomly chosen keys, and command Linda and Leslie, "Okay, everyone say all the words you can think of that start with the letter, ummm, 'P'!"

Despite Michael's busy schedule with R.E.M., he also found time to compete in the open-mike nights at The Last Resort. At one, Michael sang the Yardbirds' "Tired of Waiting," but he lost to Joe Kuhl, his upstairs neighbor at 169, who sang Dylan's "Like a Rolling Stone." At another open-mike night at Abbott's, a local pizza joint, Michael tied rags around his wrists and recited his lyrics while his sister Cindy translated into sign language.

Michael Stipe did many things—poetry, painting, photography—but it was his singing with R.E.M. that got him a hit. He did moves on stage that blew everyone away and made them think twice about the quiet, pouting prettyboy. On stage, as the music sank and soared, Michael hip-jerked and whiplashed his own body, shook and sang and begged and pleaded until at the end of a night both he and the crowd were sure that he was a star and he was sure that he had done something no one else in town was doing. And at the end of the night he went home after thrashing for hours on stage at Tyrone's or the 40 Watt, groaning with a sore back, and Linda and Leslie would lay him out on a hard flat door and watch over him while he recovered, rubbing tiger balm onto his still-spasming and twitching and lick-needing back.

Bill and Mike were enjoying the rising success of their band, but they didn't feel the need to practice styles as Michael did: They were naturals. Instinctively they could play together and lay down a rhythm section far superior to any in town. But they did need to practice styles of dressing, Michael believed. Bill sat behind the drums, so he could get away with shorts and a tank top. But Mike, little boy-looking and eyeglass-wearing, was a different story. Michael trusted the style decisions of Peter, whose costume of loose, French-cuffed shirt, black vest, black jeans, and Beatle boots was cutting edge retro. But Michael, whose early favorite performance dress was T-shirt and tennis shoes, made Mike show him the clothes he planned to wear before each date. Mike wasn't too offended; he figured being criticized by Michael was the price of success.

And it was a cheap price to pay, considering the degree of success R.E.M. was achieving. By the spring of 1981 R.E.M. was the best band in town. Pylon was still highly respected; they were the band of choice for critics. Pylon's fans were fiercely loyal and they always filled the clubs when Pylon played. But it was R.E.M. that packed the dance floors and served as a crossover band between the art school-derived scene and the rest of campus. R.E.M. was the first band to make the scene a money-making proposition by bringing the mainstream students into the clubs.

R.E.M.'s music wasn't intellectual or esoteric. It was physical, passionate. They played rock and roll with the erotic, raw energy that has defined the genre for fifty years. Mike Mills paced and hopped, matching his lyrical bass to Bill Berry's pounding. The beat was compulsive, danceable, strong. Peter Buck strutted with his guitar and leapt like Pete Townshend, grinding out primal chords and picking his top strings to sound like a music box. But Michael Stipe was the main attraction. As front man, he did a demon take that drove a crowd wild: He spun and thrashed, sweated and wailed, hanging onto the microphone as his legs gave out. His distinctive move came during the crescendos that were present in nearly all of their most popular songs like "Radio Free Europe," "Gardening at Night," "Sitting Still": He lifted and jerked his shoulder like a hooked fish above water. His body became a bullwhip, his chest a drum, as he pounded himself while he sang, pinched his nose, and slurred his neo-beat poetry in a desperate husky choke like a man expelling demons by lashing himself until his clothes hung torn from his wet frothy body.

R.E.M. had quickly convinced everyone in Athens and Atlanta that they were the best in town. Now they set out to prove it to the rest of the country. With Jefferson handling the door receipts and everyone sharing driving duty (except Michael), R.E.M. embarked on a tour of American pizza parlors and gay discos-with-New-Wave-Nights to show the country what was vital in rock in the 1980s.

Peter Buck described their early touring to *Melody Maker:*

"We'd pull into some town and if we were lucky we'd open for the local hotshit band and blow the fuckers off the stage.

"In our own naive way, we were kinda arrogant. We were

like headhunters. Sometimes we'd open for some cool bands, but usually we opened, you know, for just some nobodies who weren't very good and we'd go in and say, 'Man, let's blow them off stage.' The whole idea was to walk on and do like a fifty-minute set that was like a hurricane blowing off the stage.

"We wanted to present those people with something that was just undeniable. By the time we were finished we wanted them to think that everything else was irrelevant. I just loved that challenge. And we did it every night, man, in all those bars. Man, we musta played, like, two hundred bars, all over the south. We'd go in and there'd be maybe thirty people if we were head-lining on maybe a Cheap Drink Night—'cause we always tried to play Cheap Drink Nights, 'cause that would draw 'em in—and by the end of the set, we'd always be able to kinda go, 'See? Now tell your damned friends about this.' "

Their diet on the road was beer and speed; they added lunch meat to the menu if they were lucky enough to get a deli tray. Sometimes they'd get a pizza. In college towns the hosts of a show would invite the band to parties, and by the end of the night the guys would be gone, leaving the unfortunate host say-ing, "Hey, these guys just cleaned out my refrigerator. *And stole my girlfriend, too!*" While on the road Peter wouldn't take a shower, just put more store-bought grease in his hair. Back in Athens between road trips, they ate potatoes and rice. They went to Wendy's and loaded up on free crackers. They shoplifted cheese. Bill mixed rice and Cream of Mushroom soup and made it last for three days, reviving the leftovers with hot sauce and pepper vinegar swiped from restaurants. They drank free at Ty-rone's, where they ruled weekends, and promised repayment once they got their first gold record.

The reason R.E.M. was so successful in town was the same rea-son they were despised by the local art scene: They played down-and-dirty rock and roll.

If anybody from the art scene went to see R.E.M. they said

it was just to see Michael dance. At that time he was also playing with another band called Tanzplagen with Neil MacArthur and Lee Self. Lee Self blames pressure from the art kids for breaking up that band: "Michael [Lachowski] and Randy [Bewley] made Neil feel ashamed for playing rock and roll. It wasn't art. They hated R.E.M. too."

When the art-rock folk went to see R.E.M. they saw a room full of "normal" students dancing to a Monkees cover, and they were horrified. A favorite band of the art crowd was Jerry Ayers' Limbo District, whose sound was a discordant, percussive din. Limbo District was considered far better than R.E.M.: Whereas R.E.M. packed the club, Limbo District could clear the room in no time flat. The reaction to R.E.M.'s popularity was sometimes extreme. Mike Green, formerly of The Fans, saw a frat boy in the 40 Watt Club at an R.E.M. show and he swore never to return to the club again. Tom Smith, who had played around with Michael Stipe in Boat Of, an art-noise band with Carol Levy, first thought Stipe was cool, a little unfocused, but with earnest intensity. Then he saw R.E.M. and he turned against him with a vengeance. He made up T-shirts complete with illustrative caricature. It read: "A collective fist up M. Stipe's ass."

A division within the town was clear. The music scene in Athens had been founded on artistic innovation and naive experiment: The B-52's were a sui generis wacky spasm of postmodern cultural rubble-sifting. Pylon was British-flavored dance drone accented with Vanessa's idiosyncratic ranting naive vocals. The Method Actors were a dynamic two-man scream. Love Tractor was instrumental.

But R.E.M., with their ragged, vital rock, surpassed them all. And they were going to prove it.

They decided to do a single.

They had a meeting at Peter's house and planned to make another tape. Jefferson suggested calling his friend Peter Holsapple and asking him, and Peter supported him because he had heard of Holsapple and Stamey and Mitch Easter and the North

Carolina crowd. Holsapple suggested recording with Mitch Easter at his place, and they did. In April they recorded "Radio Free Europe" and "Sitting Still." They had a tape. Now they needed a label.

In the two years since The B-52's had showed the kids in Athens that it could be done, the music community had become savvy to the ways of cutting a record: Spend a couple of thousand dollars of somebody else's money on studio time, pressing and printing, and you've got a carton-full of plastic disks with sleeves that you can mail to critics and radio stations.

To a band like The Side Effects it seemed natural to record an EP with Danny Beard, who had in the past year teamed up with Peter Dyer, an Englishman whose Armageddon label distributed DB Recs in Britain. And in 1981 everyone recorded with Danny and Peter. That's just what you did: The B's did, Pylon, Method Actors, Kevin Dunn. So The Side Effects made an EP with Danny, as Love Tractor would. Everyone went to Danny Beard, eager to get a record out. Recording with Beard linked them genetically to The B-52's and Pylon, and, glowing from their reflections, got them a bit of press, a gig at CBGB's or Danceteria. But that was about it.

R.E.M. however, unique among the scene bands, went their own way, partly because they wanted to be different, and partly because Danny Beard didn't like them. They were anathema to the cool art crowd.

R.E.M. talked with Johnny Hibbert from Atlanta, who wanted to do a record label. Hibbert said he would put out their single and he offered them a contract. At that point Jefferson didn't feel like he had the right to express an opinion, so he didn't interfere with their signing with Hibbert. Bert Downs, by this time their biggest fan, told them he thought it was a bad contract. He told them it was a mistake to give away the publishing rights to their songs. And Peter Buck himself, skeptic and radical, had his own reservations. But despite that they all agreed to sign. As Peter concluded, "Fuck it. I want to get a record out!"

As they went to have the record pressed the other members of the band debated about scratching "Fuck Peter" into the master, but they decided against it.

The single came out in July 1981.

Finally, R.E.M. had a record; they had vinyl. They complained about the mastering, but they decided to release it anyway. As a celebration Peter smashed one and taped it to the wall. It was a new phase. It was real.

The single got rave reviews.

Quoting some of the critics, "Best unsigned band in the country!", Bill Berry called up his old friend Ian Copeland, who had left Paragon and gone on to start his own booking agency called FBI. As a favor to Bill FBI added R.E.M. to their list, the only band they booked that didn't have a label. Copeland knew it was only a matter of time.

Also at the beginning of 1981, the 40 Watt Club moved from the downtown corner of Broad and College to a space on Clayton Street where Rick the Printer had had the 11:11 Koffee Klub the year before, where R.E.M. had played and been shut down by the cops.

It was time for the club to move. The space downtown was getting dangerous, it was only quasi-legal anyway, and it was becoming a nuisance to the guy running the sandwich shop. Curtis Crowe had spotted a new place with a bar, stage, and dressing room, but Paul Scales was reluctant to take on the new club as a full-scale business. Curtis didn't have time to keep looking because he was out touring with Pylon. While Curtis was gone Scales decided to move the club to the place where Rick's Koffee Klub had been on Clayton Street.

Scales had gotten some money from a silent partner and had blown it on "just stuff." When the money-man called and said he was coming to check out the club he was allegedly funding, Scales said to Curtis, "Man, you've got to help me out!"

Foreign Legion, the record store Jefferson had been managing, had just closed. Jefferson loaned them the money for the first month's rent on their new space and gave them a counter and a cash register.

"Then we got some lumber and saw blades and sheetrock and a few days later had a nightclub," Curtis remembers. "It wasn't beautiful, but it was a club. We stole the toilets, got the wood from Tyrone's—they were tearing out their old stage and we paid some old black guy five bucks to haul it for us. Pylon opened the new Watt. I put in fifteen hours that day. Pylon was doing sound-check for the show and we were still hammering and painting. I would run up and play drums for a bit and go back to hammering some more nails. We didn't get one toilet working that night, that was the biggest problem.

"At the last minute we thought, 'Oh shit, there's no stage lights.' People were already showing up and it was the last minute so we took a lightbulb and put it into a piece of stove pipe, painted it black, and hung it up there with a coat hanger. It stayed there for years."

23

THE NEW COFFEE CLUB — OH-OK — THE B-52'S CRISIS

One day during the summer of 1981 Michael Stipe and Leslie Michel were walking along Prince Avenue on their way to Barber Street from downtown when they saw that the Ladies Auxiliary Food Bank was relocating. The food bank was housed in the bottom level of a two-story brick building behind the Coca-Cola bottling plant. The ladies were moving their stock of soup cans and rice to a cheaper vacancy next door. Michael and Leslie stopped to look.

"Wow! Cool!" Michael said as he pressed his nose and lips against the dirty storefront windows of the emptying space, squinting against the glare and rolling his cheek on the cool glass.

"This is neat!" Leslie said as she too looked in at the rough walls and bare cement floors.

They snuck in the side door marked "Service Entrance" and climbed the stairs to the second floor. They walked around the huge empty room and saw a shower and a bathroom. They found out from the ladies at the food bank that the rent was only two hundred dollars a month and it gave them an idea.

Leslie was happy living on Barber Street but, like everybody, she was always looking for a change. Something else to do. When she and Michael got back to the house at 169 they started talking about the space they had seen. First Michael suggested that he build a cardboard homestead on the second floor, a maze and refuge of found boxes, a bedroom labyrinth, a functional installation; Leslie could live downstairs. But they found out that despite the showers and bathroom the building wasn't zoned residential, and Michael reluctantly gave up the idea of the cardboard homestead.

Then Leslie realized that Athens had been without a coffee club since the cops shut down Rick the Printer's 11:11 the year before when R.E.M. played there. She thought it would be great to open her own club. She practically had one going in the kitchen of her apartment at 169 anyway. But here she could charge for coffee and cover some of the expenses.

She sat down the next day, drank some espresso, and thought of all the things she could do with a coffee club. She kept thinking, "Gotta do it! Gotta do it!" She could put on art shows. "Gotta do it!" She could have huge parties. "Gotta do it!" And she could have bands play. "It's done!" She borrowed Linda Hopper's tuition money and put down a deposit on the space. She used her own Sears credit card and charged gallons of Jungle Green bright paint. She decided on green because her medium had told her that the spirits loved green and she wanted the spirits to inhabit her club so everyone would be happy and do good and wonderful magic. She fixed the place up and called it The Night Gallery.

The next night, Oh-OK played at the opening party. Oh-OK had been started by Linda Hopper, Michael Stipe's sister Linda, and her boyfriend David Pierce. Michael had been taking seventeen-year-old Linda to parties and had encouraged Linda Hopper to play with her in a band. Linda and Linda had first rehearsed with Ingrid Schorr, for whom R.E.M.'s Mike Mills had written "Don't Go Back to Rockville." When the three personalities failed to mesh, Linda Stipe recruited David. He had recently been turned down for a drumming slot with Love Tractor after they'd advertised to replace Bill Berry, who had decided to concentrate all his energies on R.E.M.

With Linda Stipe on bass, David on drums, and Linda Hopper singing and playing the saw, they wrote some songs, and a week later they debuted their six-song repertoire while opening for Michael Stipe's solo project called 1066 Gaggle O' Sound, during which he played his Farfisa to the accompaniment of recorded noise.

When Oh-OK played they discovered they had a cute little sound that worked. They were quirky child-rock: Linda's simple bass, Hopper's shy vocals, Pierce's tiny drum. In July, after they had only played a couple of local shows, Michael Lachowski invited Oh-OK to go to New York with Pylon. Oh-OK stayed at Linda Hopper's parents' house in Baltimore on the way up. Linda told them they were on their way to see some museums for school. She hadn't told her parents yet that she was no longer taking classes but was in a band. They wouldn't have been happy. Luckily, her parents didn't say anything about the drums tied to the roof of the car.

In New York The B-52's, who frequently attended the shows of visiting Athens bands, were in the middle of recording their third album *Mesopotamia* with David Byrne. The B's brought Byrne to the show and when Linda and Linda saw him in the crowd backstage, they flipped out, screaming and gasping, "Is it really him? Is it? *It is!*"

The ebullient mood of the members of Oh-OK was a marked contrast to that of The B-52's. The thrill of seeing long-worshiped stars for the first time was an innocent joy they had lost three years earlier. By 1981 they were stars themselves. Unfortunately, they were stars that many felt had begun to lose luster, to dim, to fall.

The B-52's were having a crisis:

"The writing between *Wild Planet* to *Mesopotamia* was a real difficult period," Keith Strickland recalls. "The honeymoon was over. The fascination with being in a band, being successful— we'd already done it by that time. And at a level far beyond what we expected. We'd bought a house in Mahopac and were all living there together. And that created a strain on us, all living in one house together. In 1980 we'd done like nine months of touring and we were overwhelmed, overworked, just kind of worn out with the whole thing. We were ready for a rest. It had really become work and the fun and spontaneity of it was gone. Definitely gone.

"After *Wild Planet,* our second album, we felt pressure, that real pressure to come up with another album, and it was difficult for us to write for *Mesopotamia.* Individually we were fighting for our own space. In a way, we were tired of being The B-52's. We really needed a vacation from it. So it was difficult for us to come up with *Mesopotamia.* There was pressure to come up with something different, yet the same, and that's something you really can't do.

"We really felt in exile. We weren't in Athens. We really didn't have any friends up there. We were really like on another planet. It was a weird period. We really needed a community at that time and we didn't have one except ourselves. We were on our own. We were largely pressured by our manager [Gary Kurfurst] to do something different. He suggested working with David Byrne, although none of us were very comfortable with the idea."

Their worries were justified. *Mesopotamia* came out. Got slagged. Disappeared.

In August 1981, the music scene in Athens got its first serious attention from *The Atlanta Journal/Constitution.* It was ominous coverage; they'd finally been discovered by the mainstream press.

In a huge spread the writer surveys the town and reports its status, and wonders at the reason for it all:

"Well, how could all this come out of the home of Poss' Barbecue, the Budwine soft drink and the Dawgs? [Vic] Varney credits the town's relaxed, liberal atmosphere. 'It's the only place I've ever seen where everything in the culture is conducive to making everyone lift themselves up.'

"More important for musicians, [Michael] Lachowski says, is that 'Athens is such a cheap place to live.' "

The reporter writes:

"It's rare that where a band comes from takes on nearly as much importance as what it's playing. Michael Lachowski, Pylon's bassist, thinks the element of surprise is responsible for the worldwide attention Athens has received. . . .

"Hailing from Athens 'definitely helps,' says R.E.M. guitarist Pete Buck. . . . 'You won't get a second job some place just because you're from Athens if you're not good. But people will say, "They're from Athens, let's give them a chance." There's a lot less initial trouble getting jobs than for, say, Atlanta bands.' " In the next few years many Atlanta bands would take that to heart and relocate to Athens to take advantage of the geographical blessing.

The headline on a sidebar to the feature pegged another Athens characteristic: "No musical training is one way to sound fresh." In that sidebar Vic Varney reveals the essence of Athens' Golden Age, when he explains to the reporter: "When I left to go to Europe in April . . . nobody who's in Oh-OK even had an instrument or knew how to play. They went with Pylon to New York and played at the Peppermint Lounge on their second gig ever. There's this absolutely incredible naiveté here about the possibilities of life on Earth. I don't know why we're so arrogant or stupid to think we can do the things we do, but we do."

24

R.E.M. RECORDS 'CHRONIC TOWN' — R.E.M. SIGNS WITH I.R.S. — R.E.M. RULES

The club was dark, rowdy, dangerous, and populated with the best New Orleans had to offer: gay men in thin-lapeled jackets and ruby slippers, shag-headed women with bleary eyes, and stringy-haired junkies who only came to New Wave Night at The Beat Exchange because they could buy heroin in the back, and needles behind the bar. Few cared that the featured act that March night was the truest garage band working the East Coast: those four lovable mop-heads from Athens, Gee-A—R.E.M.

Peter Buck, his ragged-cut black hair sticky-stiff with lemon juice and road dirt, leaned against the bar taking it all in and scowling at the crowd's oblivious, uncaring mood. A woman behind the bar wiped beer suds from the cooler and bemoaned her recent bad luck. "Oh, I've had so many problems lately," she shouted above the house music. "Last week I had to fire a guy because he was selling needles and junk over the counter. But thank goodness that's all taken care of."

Peter sucked on a long-neck Bud and stared at the woman. "Lady, I hate to break it to you, but in the bathroom there are works stuck in the wall and a whole fistful of 'em clogging the toilet."

The woman exclaimed like an exasperated mother concerned, "Oh, damn! Not again! Those boys!"

It was another show on the road, but this one was a little different. For a couple of months earlier R.E.M. had been talking about record deals, entertaining the curious interest that followed the surprising popularity of their muddy little power pop single from the summer before. They'd met a few record company reps. Talked some stuff. Nothing definite. And when they hit New Orleans they were told that a representative from I.R.S. records might show up to see them play at The Beat Exchange.

They went on and played to a crowd preoccupied with scoring dope. To most of the audience the band was background noise, an ambient din, and so the band played without connecting, without their performance rising to something special. After the show the band members sat around the dressing room, drying their sweat, drinking their beers. Michael was quiet, slightly disappointed in their performance and the lackluster audience. "That sucked tonight," he said. "I'm glad the record company guy didn't come."

As if on cue, a young lanky man walked into the dressing room. "Hi," he said. "I'm Jay Boberg from I.R.S."

Peter chuckled at their fate, saying, "Aw, man, I was afraid you were going to say that. We were hoping you didn't make it."

But Boberg surprised them all. "No way, man, you guys really blew my mind tonight. It was great!" He liked them. He wanted to sign them. They had got what they wanted; they were almost there.

The previous fall, on the tail of their single, R.E.M. had recorded some songs for an EP. They had enough material for a full-length album, but the band wanted to take things one step at a time. While they checked out record deals they planned to release the EP by themselves, on Dasht Hopes, the name Jefferson had made up for a playtime promo company during his earlier romping days in Chapel Hill. Jefferson's friend David Healy, who was spending a furious but brief few months in Athens, had coopted the name to use for a label and promised to put up the money.

"When it got time to do the EP we already had worked at Mitch's for a day, but it was still kind of like we'd never been in a studio," Pete Buck recalls. "We didn't understand it. So this time we said we're going to learn recording. I would say, 'What's a tape loop?' and Mitch would show us what a tape loop was, and I'd say, 'Let's put it in this song,' and Mitch would do it. The whole time, we'd say, 'What is this?' and 'What is this?'

"We spent three days on it and got eight songs. There's everything on those cuts. I'd put like ten guitars down and compress it to one track and Mitch would dig it and say, 'This is fun.' He was having a great time. We stayed at Mitch's house that his grandmother had left him where he lived. The studio was in his Mom and Dad's house. We slept on the floor. He was real cool about it all. He realized we were broke and so we would get a pizza and he'd chip in more than his share. And Mrs. Easter liked us and she would say, 'Wouldn't you boys like some donuts?' And we'd go, 'Donuts! Hell yeah, *snarf, snarf.*' "

While R.E.M. was at Mitch Easter's the band also recorded "Ages of You" and "Shaking Through." A couple of weeks later, back in Athens, they wrote "Wolves, Lower." When David Healy, the alleged money-man, heard it, he said, "I love that new song 'Wolves,' it's gotta be on the EP." So the band said, "Sure, as long as you're paying for it." So they drove back up and recorded it.

"Then David freaked out," Peter says. "We called him once and said, 'David, the van broke down and we don't have any money.' He had wanted percentages and everything and so we said, 'You gotta give us a couple hundred dollars to get home.'

He said, 'No way, I can't do that.' So that's why he's credited on the EP as ex-producer. We got back home and fired him."

The band got Curtis Knapp, the friend of The B-52's who had helped that band get their early New York dates, to take their pictures and help with the mechanicals of the EP cover. Michael and the rest of R.E.M. did not want a picture of four guys with haircuts and pointy shoes gracing their cover. Michael wanted something to hint at the gloom and murk that was conjured by his image and the indecipherable lyrics. He wanted a gargoyle. He got it.

R.E.M. had the cover designed and the songs recorded. They were prepared to put out their EP, which Michael had named *Chronic Town*, by themselves if they had to. Then Jay Boberg walked into The Beat Exchange in New Orleans.

Leading up to that, Bill Berry had been sending R.E.M. tapes to Ian Copeland, his old friend from Macon who now ran F.B.I., the booking agency. Ian told him, "Bill, you're good. I guarantee you're going to get a record contract." To show his faith Ian added R.E.M. to his list, and they became the only unsigned band that he represented. Ian also asked the band what record label they wanted to be on. They said, oh, not a big one, maybe I.R.S. Ian said, "Good. That's my brother's label. I'll mention it to him." Miles Copeland ran I.R.S. Ian ran F.B.I. Their brother Stewart was in The Police. Their father had been career C.I.A.

"Mark Williams did most of the work," Jefferson remembers, "but Ian did mention to Miles that there was this band I want you to check out." Mark Williams had been working for A & M, I.R.S.'s distributing label, as a college rep in Atlanta, where he DJed at the 688 club and had a show on WRAS, the campus station for Georgia State. Williams told Jay Boberg, president of I.R.S., to check them out. "They have a hundred songs," Williams told him. "And they're great live."

R.E.M. decided the best approach they could take would be to sign with a small label. "Someone like us on a big label didn't make any sense," Peter says. "We'd only taken one publicity photo in our life and if we didn't feel like playing it would be, like, 'Fuck you.' It didn't matter if it was a showcase. If we felt like dicking off, we would dick off. And there's nothing wrong with that.

"If we had gone with Columbia or Warner Bros., they would have put us on the bottom line of a big showcase. We didn't see the point of going with someone who didn't understand what we were doing. We wanted someone small who would let us learn. And the way we did it, we went from being pretty bad, to being okay, to being pretty good with some problems, to being a good band.

"I'd always read too much and seen too many bands get taken advantage of, and you realize we know better what we're doing than anyone else and you've gotta kind of sink or swim with what you believe is right, and I could never let someone tell me what to do or what to record. So yeah, we turned down money and things in order to get control over what we did. We got a little better royalty rate, so it probably paid off in the long run. You know, most bands go for the fifty- or hundred-thousand-dollar advance so they can quit their day jobs and not have to tour. With us, I think we got five thousand dollars to buy drum cases and amps and make sure we travel, and we stayed on the road and stayed autonomous pretty much."

Bert Downs was at that point serving as the band's attorney. He and Jefferson connived to get back the publishing rights for "Radio Free Europe" and "Sitting Still" from Hib-Tone Records owner Johnny Hibbert. They told him they would never use those songs again if he didn't sell them back. He needed the money, so R.E.M. reclaimed two of their best songs for two thousand dollars.

R.E.M. signed with I.R.S. in May.

Chronic Town was released in August.

Finally, they would play New York City.

■ ■ ■

"Touring was where we grew," Bill Berry explains R.E.M.'s strat-
egy of building grassroots support. "At that time, nobody wanted
to play the kinds of bars we played. All these other bands didn't
want to play these sleazy places in the South. So just by us going
to these places, just by being an out-of-town band that played
this new kind of music, we were stars. People would look at us
and say, 'Wow, thanks man.' For a long time, the bands that
would open for us would be these heavy metal cover bands. So
even before we walked on stage, these little protopunks were so
grateful we were there in their towns. That's how we got so
much confidence.

"*Chronic Town* was out before we started regularly playing
New York," Bill continues. "All the art bands went to New York.
They played Athens and they played New York and they came
back and they were cool. They were written about in *New York
Rocker* and that was fine. It wouldn't have worked for us. In that
atmosphere, we couldn't go up there, say, 'Hi, we're from Ath-
ens,' and then play 'Steppin' Stone.' It just wouldn't have worked.
We didn't want to go play some showcase at Jim Fouratt's disco
at two-thirty in the morning and then go to a bunch of parties.
It just wasn't R.E.M.

"But two years later we had all this road experience and we
were a good band."

After R.E.M. signed with I.R.S., the hard-line art crowd intensi-
fied their muttering about the upstart kids who were surpassing
anything that had come before. Their previous feelings of su-
periority began to turn into bitter attacks.

"Occasionally you'd hear stuff from the trendy hangers-on,"
Peter Buck says, "and they were the assholes—a lot of the people
who were around Pylon or around The B-52's, and maybe were
their friends. I got it all the time, 'Ugh! You're a pop band!' And
I didn't see anything wrong with that. As long as it wasn't dumb.
And it wasn't dumb. We were bad, but we were never dumb. We
were younger for one thing—a lot younger. And we also were a

rock-and-roll band. But the real people involved, Vic Varney, the B's, the people in the bands here, they were always nice and involved and helpful. It was the hangers-on who were mouthing off. Waiters and waitresses studying art: 'Well! They're just certainly not artistic!' There was that dumb broad in town, didn't have a chin and always danced funny, she moved to New York and was telling everyone, 'Now that they've signed their record contract, I know they have no artistic integrity left.' And she would say that, and it would be, like, 'Hey, we have more artistic control than most bands in Athens.

" *'We can do whatever the fuck we want!'* "

25

LOVE TRACTOR — THE SIDE EFFECTS — OH-OK — THE METHOD ACTORS — NONE CAN COMPARE TO R.E.M. — BACK AT HOME, THE GIRLS WAIT

Nineteen-eighty-two was an active year for Athens bands. In January Tyrone's—the favorite club of the new bands, where R.E.M. ruled weekends—burned down. Love Tractor recorded an LP for Danny Beard, featuring Alfredo Villar, late of the ill-fated Fans, on synthesizer. Their debut, *Love Tractor*, was released in February. The record was favorably reviewed, but failed to garner anything more than limited college radio airplay, some club dates, and a handful of "Wow, swell" reviews. The Side Effects, who had the year before released a well-received EP on DB Recs called *The Side Effects*, broke up after playing a final show at the 40 Watt Club in May.

Oh-OK had done minimal touring in the fall of 1981 and in October of that year the trio recorded a four-song "mini-album," also on the Atlanta DB Recs label. In the spring of 1982 Oh-OK's "Wow Mini Album" was released and the band went on the road to play New York and Boston. "We're going up north to play three dates soon," Linda Stipe told the local college newspaper. "And after that we're going to make records and records and records."

Oh-OK started out strong. Their mini-album received high praise. The songs—all about hairdos and recess, incest and jealousy—were themes straight out of the bedrooms and off the front porches of Barber Street. Their image was kids at play, and their sound was kids untrained. *Trouser Press* described the songs as "all delivered with the simplicity of jumprope doggerel. Oh-OK pulls it off quite well. Athens is go! And Oh-OK are Hey, Neat."

The Village Voice reviewed an Oh-OK show at New York City's Danceteria in June. The reviewer noted that, coming from Athens, the band gets "unnatural attention and swanky gigs and the automatic stigma of arty-party cutes . . . but Oh-OK is charming, gentle and infectious. . . . Another Athenian alchemical reworking of the tiny, hidden formulas of pop, with no concessions to kitsch either. Thesis: Oh-OK take the radical deconstruction of rock 'n' roll that The B-52's initiated to its farthest extreme by liquidating all chords—no guitars, no keys. The result is eerie, unsettling even in its pretty, furious quietness, just melody and pound." Robert Christgau, in his consumer guide that fall, described the members of Oh-OK as having "tiny little voices and sharp little minds."

As these young bands—R.E.M., Love Tractor, Side Effects, Oh-OK—released their homemade records with their hand-carved sounds, the older bands like The Method Actors and Pylon began to feel the strain of time.

In January 1982 *Melody Maker* reviewed The Method Actors' *Little Figures* double album and hailed it as "great stuff." In March *New Musical Express* featured a favorable article about The Method Actors, titling their profile, "A Brainy Night in Georgia." In England, and in small corners of New York, L.A., and Boston, The Method Actors were highly respected and admired for their bravado at sustaining a two-man act. But back in Athens The Method Actors played to empty clubs. They hardly attracted a crowd of twenty, all of whom were old-time scene-makers and personal friends of the two musicians. Later that year, Vic and David played a brief tour in California. When they came back to Athens they played to the smallest crowd ever. Bitter, frustrated, they saw a young crowd coming up looking for something accessible. They decided to abandon their two-man act. But despite some personnel additions over the next year, The Method Actors never recovered their original cachet. David Gamble left first. Soon after that Vic too lost his motivation and dissolved the band. The Method Actors were gone.

In stark contrast to The Method Actors' misfortune and the re-spected yet weakly received efforts of Love Tractor, The Side Effects, Oh-OK, and a handful of new high-hoping quick-mix bands, R.E.M. was riding the crest of a wave that showed no sign of crashing. They crisscrossed the country in support of *Chronic Town*, playing a different town every night of the week. By late fall Jefferson's black briefcase was bulging with a thick stack of carefully clipped newspaper reviews, one from each town they played. Their press kit swelled with love notes and delirious ho-sannas.

In October 1982 R.E.M. nearly sold out the thousand-seat Agora Ballroom in Atlanta, which national acts at the time were having a hard time doing. In November R.E.M. opened for Squeeze and The English Beat at the Nassau Coliseum on Long Island. It was their biggest crowd yet: thirteen thousand. They expressed doubt about their readiness, but only playfully; they couldn't wait. "I'm going to try to make eye contact with thir-teen thousand people in forty minutes," Michael Stipe explained to a reporter before the show.

"I wouldn't want to do a tour like that," Peter Buck said, "but it's kind of irresistible to do it once. When you think about it, that's almost as many people as have bought our record so far. What if they all went out and bought the records and dou-bled the sales?"

Their innocent humility was counterbalanced by an asser-
tiveness, as their comments about fellow Athenians The B-52's
made it into print when R.E.M. turned down an opportunity to
open for the original Athens band. "Six thousand people waiting
to hear 'Rock Lobster' is not really what we want," Mike Mills
explained.

R.E.M. distanced themselves from the Athens scene to avoid
being caught up in a widely anticipated "Athens Backlash." The
propaganda about Athens had been widespread for the past three
years, and everyone felt it had been going on for too long. Like
any bull market, the Athens exchange was expected to crumble
soon. But those considerations aside, R.E.M. found it easy to
deny Athens because of the historic antagonism between themselves and the art crowd.

"We're not a party band from Athens," twenty-two-year-old
Michael Stipe declared to *Rolling Stone*. "We don't play New
Wave music, and musically, we don't have shit to do with The
B-52's or any other band from this town. We just happen to live
here."

"I don't think any of the Athens bands would have been any
different if they hadn't come from Athens," Peter Buck said.
"Everything is a little bit different, but I don't think there's any
real formative thing about Athens. It's just a place where people
play in bands."

Back in Athens, "where people play in bands," Jefferson had
moved the R.E.M. office from his apartment at 169 Barber Street
around the corner to a big yellow house on Grady Avenue where
he and Sandi Phipps lived with Peter Buck. Sandi and Jefferson
had met two years earlier on the December night that John Len-
non was shot, that tragic night when all through the neighborhoods and at the 40 Watt Club doom-drunk girls danced off their
grief and broke store windows with rag-wrapped fists. Sandi and
Jefferson were both visiting Bill Berry's house when the news
broke and together they left and wandered through the streets,
finding themselves at the end of the night in the graveyard by

the river. The two met and moved in together, and Sandi began assisting Jefferson in the band's management, as she would continue to do for the next six years. From the beginning Sandi also served as the band's unofficial photographer, shooting the portraits for use on album covers, posters, and publicity photos. After she organized the R.E.M. fan club she designed mail-outs and postcards that uncannily anticipated the haphazard, naivist style of Michael Stipe.

When the band went out of town Sandi was left to answer the mail, the phones, take messages. Together she, Ann Boyles, Linda Hopper, Lauren Hall, and Kathleen O'Brien—the R.E.M. wives—hung out during the hot summer and steaming fall of 1982, waiting for the boys to come back to town. And they found solace in the company of R.E.M.'s biggest fan, their lawyer Bert Downs.

"Whenever the band would go out of town, Bert would come take us out," Sandi remembers about those days when she was one of the wives left behind. "We would sit on his front porch on Prince Avenue all night. He would buy us flowers. One time The Replacements came through town and they stayed at the house on Grady. The band was out of town and Bert knew that I was freaked out because they were tearing everything up. Paul Westerberg kept apologizing again and again because they had destroyed the house. We came home and there were records everywhere and the beds were all torn up and I was like, 'God damn it!', crying and screaming, and Bert tried to calm me down. He kept saying, 'I'm sorry, Sandi. I'm sorry. I know it's awful.' "

26

A PHOTOGRAPH IS TAKEN — R.E.M. RELEASES 'MURMUR,' THEIR FIRST ALBUM — A COLD WIND BLOWS THROUGH ATHENS

Set on a pedestal in the middle of Broad Street in downtown Athens, the old memorial to the local Confederate dead was usually left undisturbed except by passing tourists who once in a while snapped their own take-home postcards of the obelisk, and the occasional lover or homeless desperado who used the centrally located monument as a trysting place or preaching pulpit. But on a day in December 1982 the Confederate memorial, a solemn and still tribute to the noble dead soldiers of a dead lost cause, became the focal point of yet another buzz about the whiptail doings of the local scene.

From out of the hollow rooms and littered chambers where they napped and practiced, fed and dreamed, sexed and lied, the members of Athens' steadily growing music community crawled, coordinated by café rumor, and rendezvoused at the Confederate memorial. They came carrying playtoys, guitars, horns, and hats. They came wearing scarves, jackets, sunglasses, and bluejeans; baggy pants, tennis shoes, boots and Chinese slippers: they came: members of Pylon, The Squalls, Limbo District, Kilkenny Cats, Art in the Dark, Little Tigers, Love Tractor, Oh-OK—they came when they heard what was going on. They came fast. And when they got there to that island in the middle of main street, they saw that it was true. What they had heard was true. And when they saw, the word went out louder still, to all who hadn't yet heard.

This time it wasn't a party, wasn't a new band, wasn't some who-did-who scandal. This time it was something more ominous, more foreboding than ever before reported.

"There's a photographer in town! At the Confederate memorial!" the word went.

Photographers had been visiting Athens for nearly three years since the first appearance of The B-52's—intrepid Yankee scouts visiting these alien southern lands, shooting the curiosities they'd heard rumors of, reporting on the queer dietary habits and liquor preferences of a generation of willful insomniacs. So a photographer from out of town was nothing new.

"But he's from a major national magazine!"

No big deal. Bigger than *New York Rocker*?

"But the magazine! You'll never guess!"

So who was it?

"It's *People*!"

Yagh!

Sure enough, a photographer from *People* magazine had found his way to Athens, assigned to get a picture of the scene for an upcoming issue on the resurgence of American rock. His idea was simple, graphic, and ultimately frightening. He put out the call and had all the local musicians from the new music bands gather in the middle of Broad Street, posed around the Confederate memorial. And by the afternoon, when the sun was at the photographer's back, the kids had gathered: forty folk representing twelve bands: flashbulb freaks, publicity junkies. And that wasn't all of them, just the ones who'd heard and dropped everything and run to cluster in the main street median and grab for glory. Forty was a large number, but that wasn't even all there was. Others were unavailable, but they were snubbing the furor. And R.E.M., the best of all, was out of town.

The full-page photograph appeared in the January 17, 1983 issue of *People*. It signaled the start of that significant year: the year that would see the end of the beginning: the year that closed the Golden Age of Athens.

"The white truck glides through the streets of Athens. Inside, the crew from Channel Five is doing a report on The Scene. *People* magazine has already come and gone. Seemingly, by all Media definition, Athens is the place to be this year." So reported a writer for *Muzik*, Atlanta's new music magazine, which itself had sent a contingent of writers to Athens to file stories from "smack downtown in the middle of What's Happening."

The writers from Atlanta visited the 40 Watt, hung out in the studios of some new bands, watched the students on the street, the hard-charged dancing in the clubs, and reluctantly concluded that despite their Atlanta loyalties, they had to admit that the Athens music community had offered a "renewed vitality" to rock and roll.

Of course, to balance the hype, acerbic Atlanta music critic David T. Lindsay countered the begrudged accolades with his jaundiced assessment of America's hippest college town:

"The facade is elegant nineteenth-century brownstone," Lindsay wrote. "Inside, the crumbling walls stink of rot, refuse and art rock. Syphilitics, lymphatic dead beats, idiots and rat-bitten children compete for the rock spotlight. . . . It's a place to dump the human garbage, a very private world of nepotism in a universe whose dimensions are the size and thickness and length of old guitar straps; where girls frequently soak the sidewalks in anticipation of Stipe. These people are caught in the quicksand of Athens, a depopulated alleyway of cheap diners and crummy bars. . . . The 'Athens Sound' is still merely misunderstood doublespeak for No Talent."

When the writers find longtime veterans to quote, they discover that the consensus among Athenians themselves is that the "true" scene happened two or three years earlier, when The B-52's were first rocketing out of town, when the 40 Watt was located in Curtis Crowe's loft, when Pylon was playing parties, when Michael Stipe still wore tennis shoes and T-shirts, when Peter Buck could only play chords. "The vast majority of people don't know that they are in the center of attention," one character said. "Those that do know would rather the rest of the world not find out."

That was a futile wish. The horses had bolted. The stable doors would not shut.

Three months after the publication of the full-page, all-star, wow-sensation *People* magazine photograph of the Athens, Gee-A, glory-hounds, R.E.M. released their first full-length LP: *Murmur*. April 12, 1983, the release date, clipped the back end of the period that began with the *People* photo in January: three months during which the Athens scene was allowed to slowly/quickly adapt itself to the fact that it was no longer a cult sensation, and was now a full-fledged, mainstream, national object of fascinated obsession. The legacy of The B-52's had primed the lust for attention, and the January *People* photograph had tickled the town and thrown the scene into a tizzy—but it was the April release of *Murmur* that delivered to the scene the pro-wrassling equivalent of a piledriver, stunning it cold.

That moment in the history of the Athens scene was unprecedented. Other albums had come out of Athens before: The B-52's first three albums, Pylon's *Gyrate*, The Method Actors' *Little Figures*: and they were all highly praised, all recognized as significant contributions to the collective rock memory.

None equaled the impact of *Murmur*.

On *Murmur* R.E.M. capitalized on the mystique of the South and the sense of place and environment that it is known for, despite the fact that none of the band's members was "native" to the region. As a band, they took the standard clichés of pop rock and twisted them, convolved them through naive manipulation and quirky taste into something murky, complex, thick. Peter and Michael at first tried to find something "Flannery O'Connor-like" for the cover. They each wanted something twisted, crazy-rooted, mystical. The photo of a kudzu field on which they finally agreed perfectly represented their sound and image: tangled, blurred at the edges. And kudzu itself became R.E.M.'s ideal icon: It was everything they were: overwhelming, unstoppable, creeping, and ultimately dominating.

The music press had not been that excited in years. R.E.M. were the redeemers of American rock at a time when British synth bands dominated. They had gone beyond the easy quirk of New Wave, yet remained within the original do-it-yourself punk paradigm, adapting it to the American context: Four boys in thrift-store clothes and, at the time, shockingly shaggy hair, with no synthesizers, no guitar solos, and no hairspray—playing simple yet layered melodic pop music. Scrap was their natural environment, and R.E.M. affected a counter-commercial fashioning of a style derived from the cultural junk pile, hence their affinity with Georgia folk artist Howard Finster, the lunatic visionary junk-collecting preacher whose work was a collection of fragmented images with the power of an old man invested in it. R.E.M. was a bit of Huck Finn in Reagan's corporate neocon new-yup America. But they weren't ideologues, which was a pleasant break from the social commentary that was the theme of much folk-punk at the time.

"We were evidence that you could get by never reading a newspaper," Peter says.

The apolitical attitude of the kids at the time wasn't unanimous in town. There was a small group that published a magazine, *Line of Sight*, dedicated to the overthrow of Reaganism. There was another group that each year held a Human Rights Festival commemorating the deaths at Kent State. And there was Ed Tant, a local activist whose columns in the local paper

The Athens Observer consistently attacked social ills. Tant, a sixties radical, felt let down when the new generation spent all its
time in the clubs and not on the barricades. At bars and parties
Tant offered this insightful comment about the music scene to
anyone who would listen: "The kids these days say they started
a band. Well, I say we stopped a war! They can't tell you who
wrote *The Grapes of Wrath,* but they can tell you who's the
drummer for R.E.M.!"

Politics was far from R.E.M.'s agenda. They had rejected
ideology so heartily that they even refused to be committed to
lyrics of any sort. The words, the name, the look—it can mean
what you want it to mean, they said.

The kids loved it. It was perfect. The B's were literal, but
absurdist. Pylon was obtuse, but in a known style—a cynical, late-
seventies, proto-post-modern Talking Heads-ish ironic distanc-
ing. Everybody else at least said *something.* Michael Stipe didn't
say *any*thing. His voice was "just another instrument," and the
lyrics were strings of melodic syllables, snippets and catch phrases
of intriguing composition. They were obscure, yet suggested
some meaningful context from which they came. To the generation of a new decade, fatalistic in the face of Reaganism and
desirous of the spectacle of meaning rather than the truth of it,
R.E.M.'s obscurantism, Michael's pseudo-aphasia, was perfect.

R.E.M.'s songs gave listeners plenty of room to insert themselves as reader. Stipe was saying something, they knew, but
what? It sounded like words, but what words? And people inserted their own; they heard what they wanted to hear: "Take
your fortune" became "Take up boxing"; "We could gather
throw a fit" became "We could gather throw up beer." And,
more often than not, a singalong with *Murmur* sounded uncannily like an experience of pentacostal glossolalia.

The "chiming, ringing, jangling" guitar of Peter Buck; the
melodic bass of Mike Mills; the steady beat of Bill Berry; and the
mellifluous poetic howl of Michael Stipe was definitely special.
No doubt about that: *Murmur* made all the "Best of" lists for

1983 and R.E.M. was voted best new artist in the *Rolling Stone* Critics' Poll.

There was a tragic counterpoint to R.E.M.'s brilliant achievement. In an unnerving coincidence, on the night of *Murmur*'s release a carload of kids from Athens drove to Atlanta to see a showing of *Smithereens*, Susan Seidelman's first film featuring Richard Hell, leader of the early punk band the Voidoids. Hell claimed to be the first person to wear a torn T-shirt as punk style. Hell was a hero, and "Blank Generation" was an anthem. So when he was scheduled to appear at the screening, many attended. But on the way back the car of kids was struck from behind by a speeding car and knocked into the median, where it flipped and rolled and came to rest. Killed in the crash were Carol Levy, Michael Stipe's beloved antagonist, and Larry Marcus, keyboardist with the popular Athens band Little Tigers.

The next morning the news went around town as it always went around, but this news stunned the kids into a spring of silence and sadness. Carol Levy had been a catalyst to the scene, as inspiration, and when she was buried in Atlanta, her graveside circled with weeping mourners, something crucial to the community was buried with her, an honest, aggressive, hopeful voice. Her friends spent the summer trying to recover from the shock, furiously picking armfuls of purple-and-white bachelor's buttons, attempting to ease her passing with fresh color, and forget their own pain and loss by burying their memories in flowers picked from the roadsides and vacant lots around town. But it didn't work. The spell of innocence that had fired the first furious scene was fading, ending: And the end came swiftly:

In December Pylon, Athens' foremost party dance band, abandoned their fruitless wait for a major recording deal and broke up. Later that month, on a cold drizzly night, a pretty young woman who worked in the same building downtown where R.E.M. had recently located their new corporate headquarters, was murdered behind the Academic Building on campus, just one hundred feet from her office. She became the first person murdered on the U. of G. campus in the twentieth century. Only days later, Jimmy Ellison, formerly the bass player for The Side Effects and ex-husband of Pylon's singer Vanessa, was diagnosed with a brain tumor that would kill him within a year.

For the first time in recorded history the temperature in Athens dropped to zero degrees on Christmas day. Water pipes froze and burst, and the kids left in town over the holidays huddled bundled around the open doors of ovens and the flickering blue flames of hissing gas heaters. As the year ended a cold wind blew through America's premier college town, and *Murmur* climbed to number fifty-four in 1983's Top 100 albums.

27

THE ATHENS SHOW — THE WHOLE WORLD IS WATCHING

The posters began to appear in the first couple of weeks of February 1984, stuck in store windows, nailed to telephone poles. They read: "The Athens Show. Premiere at The Mad Hatter. Feb. 24." The posters were bigger than the usual letter-size photocopied handbills taped and tacked up around town by the usual youthful self-promoters. "The Athens Show" was a production, the first of its kind in the scene, the first attempt by a couple of local businessmen to take advantage of the commercial potential latent in the booming reputation of the once-hick, still small, now famous upland Georgia town.

"The Athens Show" was a video of Pylon's final farewell performance, shot the previous December. Both the final performance and the premiere of the video were held at The Mad Hatter, a downtown club usually patronized by frat boys and rednecks come into town from surrounding counties to see big-hair metal bands. It was a sign of Pylon's massive local popularity that The Mad Hatter was required to hold the crowd that eagerly attended both events. It was also an acute irony that Pylon's disbanding drew such support; such was the casual design of their project:

"Very few real decisions were made by Pylon," Michael Lachowski says, diagnosing the maladies and circumstances that led to Pylon's surprising breakup. "That's one of our faults. When we started, we thought it was just going to last long enough to play around some. But once we were playing clubs and making money, it was, like, 'Hell yeah!' And then when the first single came out and got publicity in New York, it was, like, 'Whoa!' And with the album *Gyrate* it was, like, 'Oh sure, why not?' Most of what happened to us, it was offered and we just went along."

The aftermath of *Murmur* left scorched earth. When the smoke cleared and the dust settled, the landscape was rearranged. Not just a few were left choking. The prominence of R.E.M.-style pop rock among the new music kids signaled doom for the old art bands; their wave was over. Pylon's second album, *Chomp*, and a new single, "Crazy," failed to win that band major label interest. By 1983 they had been together for four years and had yet to make anything more than a survival wage. Aside from the changing musical trends, the major blame for their lack of financial success fell on the independent label DB Recs. Danny Beard's operation was run out of a back room; records were kept in spiral notebooks, some say written in crayon. Plus, Danny's partner Peter Dyer was given access to monies from both the record label and Danny's record store. Danny Beard later regretted his own casual approach to running the business, after funds were spent foolishly. Danny eventually severed ties with Peter Dyer, but too late; the label was in chaos. There was little they could do for the bands. In December 1983, Pylon played their farewell show.

It was as though Pylon had a built-in obsolescence, a self-destruct mechanism that triggered when they went beyond a certain point:

"Curtis and Michael brought it up to begin with," Vanessa remembers about the break up. "It's like they were just tired of it. It was getting to be too much trouble. I told Randy that I knew I would hear this someday, I just didn't know when. I didn't want to argue to keep the band together if anyone else wanted to break it up. What good would that be? I just went along with what everyone else wanted to do. It was the best time to do it. We were still having fun. We might have actually signed with a major label. Then again, we might not have. Who knows?"

"We knew that when we quit it was going to capture people's attention," Michael Lachowski says. "Everybody thought we were 'this far' from making it, and we quit. But from our side, that was completely unknown. No one could really say we were that close. There was no evidence whatsoever. We weren't going to ask a major label to give us anything. If they didn't know we were good then they weren't going to find out. I guess we were snobbish in that regard. So we weren't going up the scale and we didn't want to stay where we were. And we weren't making people sick yet. We hadn't pissed anybody off. Compared to a lot of bands that at that time were working their butts off, we did good. We didn't sell out. And we didn't just peter out and fade away."

As 1984 began, Pylon was history. And on February 24 The Mad Hatter filled with the burgeoning numbers of students from campus who wanted to take part in an "Athens Scene" event—advertised, labeled and promoted as such. "The Athens' music scene is going Hollywood," declared a *Red and Black* article on the show. In true Athens style, before the video was shown yet another new band debuted:

It was, again, ironic and tragically fitting that Buzz of Delight opened for "The Athens Show." The main force in the two-man band was Matthew Sweet. He typified "the new Athenian." He was a prospector, come to Athens to take advantage of the town's cachet. Sweet had met Michael Stipe when R.E.M. played

Sweet's hometown of Lincoln, Nebraska. The teenager was intrigued. He began a correspondence with R.E.M.'s fan club. It wasn't long before he told his parents he was going to school at the University of Georgia, and early in the summer of 1983 he drove a Cadillac convertible into Athens, suitably armed with a precocious talent, homemade tapes, a bellyful of ambition, and a pocketful of his daddy's credit cards.

Sweet came to Athens in the summer of 1983. Unable to immediately bond with Michael Stipe, who was out of town promoting *Murmur*, Sweet took up with Linda Hopper. He soon joined Linda's band Oh-OK. Matthew then quit Oh-OK, and teamed up with David Pierce, Oh-OK's original drummer who had quit the year before. Together they formed Buzz of Delight, a name coined by Linda and Michael Stipe. Pierce and Sweet then recorded a Christmas single and an EP for DB Recs—all this before they ever played in public at their debut before "The Athens Show."

"I calculated it," Sweet admitted to a *Washington Post* reporter, when questioned about his social climbing.

After securing some New York dates, Sweet and Pierce played there. Unbeknownst to Pierce, Sweet had begun communication with some record companies. Soon he had a deal lined up for himself. Back in Athens, Sweet took Pierce aside and told him it was over: he didn't need him anymore, he had got what he wanted: a deal. The experience soured Pierce on music for a long time after. "*I was pissed!*" Pierce would say years later. And Matthew Sweet himself soon left town with an unsavory reputation.

On that night when Buzz of Delight opened for "The Athens Show," Sweet's machinations were yet to be realized. But in hindsight it can be seen that as Pylon's last show marked the end of the Golden Age, Buzz of Delight's debut marked the beginning of the next era: an era of admitted and explicit ambition, more intentional band-marketing, competition, and strategic styling. The folks would say, again and again, it was then that innocence was banished.

Love Tractor had played with Pylon on the night of that band's farewell performance, and so they also were featured in "The Athens Show." While Love Tractor was still a working band in 1984, they too suffered from an inefficient label. Like Pylon, they were frustrated, tired, disillusioned. They had recorded their DB Recs album *Around the Bend* in the fall of 1983 and it was released in early 1984. The video for the single, "Spin Your Partner," made it onto MTV, and the album got a good deal of college radio airplay, but when the band toured there were no albums in the local record stores for the newly won fans to go out and buy. Then their drummer Kit Swarz quit once again and was replaced by Andrew Carter. By late 1984 Love Tractor was considered ripe for the picking by a major label. They had added vocals to their songs and were willing to tour. But nobody was interested. It was a pattern that would repeat itself for the rest of the decade.

Unlike all the rest, R.E.M. had a good year in 1984. They released their second album, *Reckoning,* to still another wave of acclaim. The album featured an ode to the band's early touring days—"Little America"—and Michael Stipe's valediction to Carol Levy, "Camera." The album was a maturation and a departure. The band was more confident and the lyrics were gradually becoming more comprehensible. Membership in the fan club began to reach into the thousands. R.E.M. was solidly on their way to the toppermost of the poppermost.

Following each new R.E.M. album—one each year after *Murmur*—the mainstream press came back to Athens. *The Washington Post, Newsweek, Entertainment Tonight*—the reporters came to divine the scene. In 1984 the reporters looking for a story scouted the new 40 Watt Uptown, the latest version of Athens' first and quintessential new-music dive. The 40 Watt Uptown was now located in a reconstituted fern bar, complete with brass

railings and a liquor license—the better to accomodate the swelling crowds of students that now showed up to see the increasing
number of local bands as well as the national acts that were
beginning to play Athens. The one-time cow town had become
a site of prestige for touring bands, now that it was a landmark
new-rock district.

The press came, took away some freshman's quote, some
drifter's diagnosis of the movement, and went to print with the
by-then stereotyped image of Athens: an eighties Liverpool
South, a place where legions of kids came each fall, new pop fan
students filling the town, feeling the fever, starting new bands,
packing the clubs. In a few short years Athens had been trans-
formed by a handful of kids from a hick college town to a holy
shrine designed by a punk Faulkner, where rock poets in Future
Farmers of America jackets, and painted and porcelain-powdered
party babes, dance till the break of day to the sound of jangly
guitars, and wander footsore and famedrunk to first-period class
at the university—while the whole world watches. . . . It made
good copy.

"And, oh, what a scene it is," reported *The Washington Post*
in a 1984 article titled "O Little Town of Rock 'n' Roll." "Home
town of the University of Georgia Bulldogs, mecca for beer-
bellied Hairy Dawg devotees in red underwear, reputed sight of
the first streaker and the place once picked as Playboy's No. 1
Party Town, Athens is inspiring almost everyone to pick up a
guitar and get down."

It was the same a year later when *Newsweek* filed its report,
"Hot Rockin' in Athens":

"It's nearly twelve on a Friday night in Athens, Ga., and the
40 Watt Club Uptown is going strong. . . . The throng surrounding the boot-high stage starts to jump and grind, and a few
overeager leather-clads pogo and slam-dance, causing bodies to
bounce about. . . . No doubt about it, in this town, there's good
rockin' at midnight."

Flipside to the accolades was the internal bitching. "For

years it has been denied ... that there is such a thing as an 'Athens Music Scene,'" wrote one fan(atic) in *Tasty World,* a local new-music tabloid started by former Oh-OK drummer David Pierce. "But now, trendies abound in Athens. It's too late to argue about semantics. The Athens Music Scene has become a reality. . . . Hey, if you're not in a band, don't start one. Please, no more new bands. . . ." The writer went on to praise a recent R.E.M. show at Atlanta's Fox Theater with a nostalgic "so good to see the boys again" tone.

"I thought R.E.M. at the Fox sucked!" responded another fan in the next issue of *Tasty World.* "Stipe didn't dance—no enthusiasm whatsoever from the band as a whole." Then came the credentials debate, the "I knew 'em first" bitch: "Where was [the first writer] during the Tyrone's era? If she thinks the Fox show was spectacular, then she wasn't around when Tyrone's was home to this band."

The "scene": The in-crowd reluctantly used the word, but when they inevitably did they cringed and threw quotes around it. With craning neck and wagging head they hissed the word. Its pronunciation became symbolic of the bitterness that was taking root in town, as they sneered out a spitting "s," followed by a long, grating "e" sound—a nasal, mocking singsong "eeee"— and ended it with a whiplash, a stinging, whining "n."

And on it went: petulant, pissy, competitive: One night a gaggle of new musicians who had been criticized in *The Red and Black* by that newspaper's entertainment editor, Charles Aaron, conspired to attack their nemesis. They found him outside the 40 Watt and hit him with pies made from Comet, molasses, and barbecue sauce. The attack was supported by David Pierce, editor of *Tasty World,* because Pierce felt *The Red and Black* was not supportive enough of the scene: "Aaron has such a base dislike for the local music that he is only outdone by his inherent ignorance of music and lack of credibility in his writing."

In another *Tasty World* column, this one written under a pseudonym and printed right next to a picture of Aaron after the attack, Pierce himself took up the propagandizing mission he had criticized *The Red and Black* for lacking. Pierce repeated the oft-heard and, by 1985, untrue festering old saw about the quaintness and sense of community of the Athens scene, a trope that was blatantly contradicted by his championing of the pie-slingers: "Athens is no mecca or magic wonderland for artists and musicians," Pierce wrote, with blinders firmly in place, "only a small town where the pretentions of the big-city rivalry are reduced to the positivism of friendship among productive people."

Finally the scene got so bad that the movie cameras showed up. In January 1986 Subterranean Productions, a film company from Los Angeles, came to Athens to make a documentary about "the Athens scene." Their presence in town caused a flurry of rumors and whispers, as the crew was offered their pick o' the chicks and aspiring stars worked connections to be featured, as parties were held in hotels all across town and the director did handstands in Pete Buck's hallway. The result, *Athens, Ga., Inside/Out*, received mixed reviews from critics outside the state, but an almost unanimous thumbs-down from the locals in Athens itself.

As a documentary, the movie failed to cover the basics of "scene" history. While much of the footage was interesting, the historical information in the movie was inadequate; the filmmakers ignored a number of crucial characters and players in the town. The most glaring omission was Danny Beard, whose record label DB Recs was the "label to the stars" in the early days. The filmmakers paid much attention to Howard Finster, who was not an Athenian and who had had little-to-no influence on the scene up until then. They also made main characters out of Dexter Romwebber and his master-blaster, jaw-dropping, two-man band Flat Duo Jets, although Dexter had only been in town for a couple of months and was to leave town after the movie was made. The filmmakers did manage to capture an impression of Athens at that particular time, featuring performers such as Paul Lombard, Time Toy, Barbeque Killers, Kilkenny Cats, and the poet John Seawright, but it was a slice taken during a down-spell: Filmed in winter, the movie had no sweat on it; *Athens, Ga., Inside/Out* missed the summer—those nine months of skinny-dipping, iced tea, and gin-and-tonic when the folk of Athens are kids together outrageously, with nothing more important on their minds than where to buy bootleg beer on Sunday.

Ultimately, the end result of the moviemaking was to show how difficult it is to pin down what counts as "a scene." How can you measure a thing in motion? Can you tack an intangible to a board? Dissect it? Analyze it? Reproduce it? The inadequacy of the movie caused the kids to ask themselves what counts as "a scene," what is the vital ingredient. On the dance floor they get close to an answer, they feel they've got it figured out, but when they stop to explain, it evaporates like sweat from a satin party dress.

They conclude: Forget it. Just *feel* it.

28

FADE OUT

"Griel Marcus says that bands are 'images of community.' There must be something about Athens, Georgia; it seems to breed eclectics. Maybe it's the fallout from the DuPont Factory where the members of Pylon have worked; maybe it's art studies at the University of Georgia; maybe it's the laetrile in the peach pits or the sweet summer sweat. . . ."

KAREN MOLINE on Pylon
New York Rocker
March 1981

"Every story about this place begins, ' "There must be something about the drinking water in Athens,"

says Bert Downs, the R.E.M. lawyer.' People also the-
orize about the air and the red Georgia clay. . . ."
RON GIVENS on Athens
"*Newsweek* on Campus,"
March 1985

Nobody ever did figure it out. Couldn't. There was nothing
to figure out. The reason Athens, Georgia, saw the birth of the
most notable American rock scene of the 1980s wasn't because
of the red clay, the water, or the sweat. It wasn't the cheap rent,
the art school, or the availability of beer and LSD. It was simply
the dynamic of exceptional coincidence. It was the initial coincidence that led The B-52's to meet, get drunk, play, have taste
and talent, and then themselves meet the right people at the
right historical moment and play New York when that dark town
needed a blast of color and light. Following that, there was the
coincidence that Lachowski met Bewley met Crowe met Briscoe
met Fred met Danny met Dana met Vic met Gamble met . . . .
. . . . on up to Buck meeting Stipe meeting Kathleen meeting Bill
meeting Mike meeting Jefferson meeting Sandi meeting . . . .
and on and on and continuing even today in a great chain of
begettings that has sparked up such bands as Dream So Real and
the Chickasaw Mudd Puppies. Call it coincidence or call it magic:
Whatever you call it, it wasn't the water.

EPILOGUE

The B-52's:

The B-52's, the first band of the Athens music scene, released *Whammy*, their third album, in 1983. It was considered a return to the band's original sound and style, but unfortunately the sound and style of the "tacky little dance band from Georgia" had by that time come to be seen as dated, and the band itself, which had been headquartered in New York since 1979, was considered a New Wave novelty. This was especially so in light of the rise of the new American guitar-thrash bands like The Replacements, Husker Du, and R.E.M. Ricky Wilson died from an AIDS-related ailment in 1985, and the next year The B-52's released *Bouncing Off the Satellites*, the last of their albums to feature Ricky's work. The album was dismally promoted and the band grew discouraged. Following a two-year hiatus during which the band recovered from the loss of Ricky and the disappointment of *Bouncing Off the Satellites,* The B-52's staged a totally unexpected comeback with *Cosmic Thing,* an album that is a paean to their bucolic early days in Athens, and that reached number one on the charts.

Pylon:

The members of Athens' favorite dance-party band all remained in Athens after the band's breakup in 1983, settling in to marriages, jobs, and families. Their place in the folklore of the town had been assured by their unexpected early retirement, and as the music scene grew and became more formal the new kids in town heard the stories of the "old days"—at the center of which legend was this band called Pylon. After R.E.M. recorded a version of Pylon's "Crazy" their notoriety increased. In 1988 Pylon re-formed, and their reunion attracted international attention. In 1990 they released a new album, *Chain,* and have continued to tour.

R.E.M.:

After releasing *Reckoning* in 1984, R.E.M. continued their one-way climb to the top with one album a year, each one surpassing the previous in sales: In 1985, *Fables of the Reconstruction;* in 1986, *Life's Rich Pageant;* in 1987, *Document.* It was then, in 1987, that for the first time one of their singles, "The One I Love," made it into the Top 10. That success effectively ended R.E.M.'s status as a cult band. They had attained mainstream success. In 1988 R.E.M. left I.R.S. and signed with Warner Bros. That year they released *Green* which, along with a successful year-long tour in 1989 promoting that album, solidified their place as America's best and hippest rock-and-roll band.

Love Tractor:

Despite considerable critical acclaim, Love Tractor has not achieved the popularity of either Pylon or R.E.M. Nevertheless, they have continued to tour and record. In addition to their debut *Love Tractor*, the band has also released *Around the Bend, Til the Cows Come Home, Wheel of Pleasure,* and *Themes from Venus.*

Printed in the United States
130890LV00004B/63/A